COMMISSIONERS HALL,

Northern Liberties.

HISTORY AND DIRECTORY

OF

TEMPLE PRESBYTERIAN CHURCH,

FORMERLY

CENTRAL PRESBYTERIAN CHURCH IN THE NORTHERN LIBERTIES,

PHILADELPHIA.

BY

JAMES Y. MITCHELL,
PASTOR.

J. W. DAUGHADAY & CO.,
PHILADELPHIA.
1873.

Righter & Gibson, Binders,
1214 Chestnut St.

PREFACE.

The idea of writing this history did not originate with me. By a vote of the Board of Trustees, on the 13th of April, 1868, my name was associated with others on a committee to do a work of this kind. The matter of compiling and writing was left entirely to me. Very soon after this appointment, engagements connected with the building of the "New Church" were quite sufficient to claim all the time I could reasonably give outside of my regular pastoral duties. This will account for the work being delayed until the present time. More recently our Synod took formal action looking towards the preparation of histories of individual churches, and the "Presbyterian Historical Society," through its Secretary, Mr. Samuel Agnew, has been earnest in pressing this subject upon the attention of pastors.

For much of the introductory history in this volume I am indebted to Rev. T. J. Shepherd, D.D., whose book, entitled "The Days that are Past," should be in the hands of all who are interested in the beginnings of Presbyterianism in the northern section of our city. I have also examined, in connection with our own church records, the records of other churches. I have consulted with persons in the city, and corresponded with others out of the city, for facts, or for confirmatory evidence of facts already possessed.

I have incorporated here and there, throughout the work, so much of outside history as I have felt requisite; for frequently what was going on without was the occasion of, or gave coloring to, what was going on within the church.

I am glad to believe that the work meets with the cordial approval and endorsement of those to whom it has already been submitted for examination, and can desire no more than that its publication will intensify the attachment and love of our members to this church, which God has so wonderfully kept, and so signally blessed.

JAS. Y. MITCHELL.

MAY, 1873.

HISTORY.

"We have thought of thy loving kindness, O, God, in the midst of thy temple. Walk about Zion, and go round about her: tell the towers thereof. Mark ye well her bulwarks, consider her palaces; that ye may tell it to the generation following. For this God is our God, for ever and ever: he will be our guide even unto death."

Psalm, xlviii: 9, 12, 13, 14.

CHURCH HISTORY.

I.

INTRODUCTORY HISTORY.

To The Presbyterian Church must be accorded the honor of inaugurating regular religious services in the northern section of our city.

For some time before the Revolutionary War, when all north of Vine street was nothing more than a country settlement, the Second Presbyterian Church, then worshiping at the corner of Third and Arch streets, held the "North End" of the city as a field for their missionary labors.

There was not the attraction of a dense population to call them to this work. There was no commodious or attractive room in which to gather a congregation. Love for souls, and a deep interest in the Master's kingdom, alone impelled them to it.

Uninviting as the field was, the Second Church

cultivated it. Arrangements were made for services to be held at stated times, in a small house, which they provided and fitted up, at the north-east corner of St. John and Coates streets.

The different pastors of that church fully entered into that movement, and gave of their time and talents to preach the unsearchable riches of Jesus Christ in the midst of these waste places.

In the Providence of God, these pulpit ministrations were of the very highest order. During the whole time that this was occupied as a missionary field, the Second Church was blessed with four of the very best preachers and pastors, viz.: Drs. Gilbert Tennent, James Sproat, Ashbel Green, and Jacob J. Janeway; men alike gifted, zealous, wise, warm-hearted and evangelical.

These labors, so early begun, were interrupted by the Revolutionary War.

The British army encamped here, and the house in which religious services had been held was used as a receptacle for military stores.

From this fact it received the name by which it was afterwards known—"*The Old Cannon House.*"

Soon after the termination of the "War," Rev. Dr. Sproat revived the services which had been interrupted.

The congregation soon became too large for the building they had, and, of necessity, they were led to consider the project of erecting a church building elsewhere.

A lot at the northwest corner of Second and Coates streets, was donated for this object by Mr. William Coates. Money was solicited and secured for the building. The work went on, and on Sabbath, April 7th, 1805, the completed building was opened with appropriate services.

This mission church was afterward formally organized into what is now known as the First Presbyterian Church in the Northern Liberties.

God abundantly blessed the labors which were there bestowed. He poured out copiously of His Holy Spirit upon the people, and the first pastor of the church had the pleasing satisfaction of seeing the membership grow from *fifty-two*, the number at the time of his installation, January 11th, 1814, to about *eleven hundred*, the number enrolled in the spring of 1829, when it was proposed to move to a more westward location.

The subject of removal was agitated for about three years. In March, 1832, a lot of ground was purchased in Buttonwood street, below Sixth, and in May following, the work of building a new edifice commenced.

The lecture room in the new church building was opened for service in December of the same year; and on May 12th, 1833, the audience room being finished, was appropriately dedicated to the worship of God.

The signal success which attended the preaching of Mr. Patterson, the crowds which waited on his ministry, the constant growth of the population, and the felt want of increased church accommodations, led some of his people to seek for the establishment of

ANOTHER CHURCH.

As early as the year 1825, one hundred and four persons petitioned the Philadelphia Presbytery to organize a new church.

Through their committee, the Presbytery organized a church, to be known as the "Second Presbyterian Church in the Northern Liberties."

This church called the Rev. James Smith to be their pastor, and for five years maintained worship in the Commissioners' Hall, in Third street, below Green.

At the end of that time they undertook the erection of a building in Sixth street, above Green. They succeeded in getting the building under roof, and occupying the basement for worship, but they were well-nigh overwhelmed with financial troubles.

At this time,

ANOTHER COLONY,

of thirty-eight persons, went out from the First Church.

These persons had all along differed from their brethren on the question of church site, and felt, too, that they had an independent work to do for their Master. They asked, therefore, to be dismissed, in order to constitute the "Third Presbyterian Church in the Northern Liberties."

Dismissed, and regularly organized into a church, they met for worship, conducted by Rev. Hugh M. Koontz, in a school-room on Poplar street, above Second.

In the course of a few months, negotiations for the union of the Second and Third Churches were begun and consummated.*

The plan of union provided that both of the churches should drop their names, and come together under the name of "The First Presbyterian Church of Penn Township."† The pastor of the Second Church was to resign, and Rev. H. M. Koontz, the supply of the Third Church, was to be elected pastor of the united church. The burden of completing the building was to be borne by the Third Church.

Thus united, the work of finishing the building was pushed rapidly forward.

II.

ORGANIZATION OF THE "CENTRAL PRESBYTERIAN CHURCH IN THE NORTHERN LIBERTIES."

In the "First Church of Penn Township," differences of opinion soon arose, and before the congregation had occupied the audience-room of their building, the communion was distracted and divided. One part, by common consent, retained the house, the

---

* This new organization was effected November 21st, 1831.

† This church is now called "The North Presbyterian Church."

pastor, and the name. The other part returned to the school-room on Poplar street, worshiped there for a short time, then went to "The Commissioners' Hall," in Third street, below Green.*

In the second story of this hall a church organization was effected, on June 24th, 1835, under the title of "The Central Presbyterian Church in the Northern Liberties." Rev. John McDowell, D.D., presided, and Rev. C. C. Cuyler, D.D., assisted at the organization. Twenty-one persons enrolled themselves as members of the church. These persons presented certificates of dismission to organize this new church, as follows:

From the First Presbyterian Church, Penn Township.

Charles Elliot,	Joseph Pond,
Anna Maria Elliot,	Catharine Pond,
John G. Flegel,	Hannah Harby,
Sarah Flegel,	Margaret Naglee,
Ellen Naglee,	Ann Reynolds,
Joseph Naglee,	Benjamin Naglee,
Hannah A. Naglee,	Hannah R. Naglee,

From the Fifth Presbyterian Church, Philadelphia.

John A. Stewart,	Margaret Stewart.

From the First Presbyterian Church, Northern Liberties.

William P. Aitken,	Amelia Aitken,
Joseph Aitken,	Mary M. Aitken,

Charles C. Aitken.

* This hall was torn down some few years ago, and in its place now stands the Northern Liberties Public School.

After the organization, the people elected three elders, who were solemnly set apart to their office. Agreeably to a notice given from the pulpit, June 28th, 1835, a meeting of the congregation was held on Monday, June 29th. At this meeting the congregation proceeded to an election for pastor, when a call was unanimously made out for the pastoral services of Rev. WM. H. BURROUGHS.*

Mr. Burroughs had been preaching and laboring in the Northern Liberties since the 19th of April, preceding this meeting, and with considerable success. He accepted the call of this congregation, and was installed as the *first* pastor of this church by the Second Presbytery of Philadelphia, on the evening of August 24th, 1835.

The installation services were held in the First

---

* Mr. Burroughs was born in Vermont, and educated at Hamilton College, N. Y. After leaving College, he taught for some time a classical school in Trenton, N. J Afterwards he became a teacher in the Manual Labor Institution at Germantown, Pa. When a Manual Labor Academy was instituted at Elizabethtown, N. J., he was invited to take charge of it, which he did, and continued in this position for two years, when he relinquished it, in order to give his whole attention to preparation for the ministry. He was licensed to preach the gospel by the Presbytery of Elizabethtown, February 19th, 1833. Two months later, by the same Presbytery, he was ordained to the work of the gospel ministry with a view to his laboring as a stated supply in the church at New Providence, N. J. On October 8th, 1833, he was regularly installed as pastor of that church. In the spring of 1834 he was called to the First Church, Penn Township, but his Presbytery refused to release him from his charge at New Providence. His health was greatly impaired about this time; and after a journey to the South in 1834, he returned to his charge, followed by a call from Oakland College, Mississippi, to become a Professor in that institution, also by overtures from a number of persons in the First Church, Penn Township, to come to this city and lead them in the formation of a congregation and the building of a new church. This invitation he accepted, and thus became the first pastor of this church.

Presbyterian Church, N. L., by invitation from the pastor, Rev. James Patterson.

Before this church organization, however, the people, though small in numbers, were arranging for the building of a church edifice. By mutual agreement, Messrs. Joseph Naglee, Benjamin Naglee, Joseph Pond, John A. Stewart, and John G. Flegel, met with Mr. Charles Elliot, at his house, on December 31st, 1834, to consult together "on the expediency of erecting a building, to be occupied by a Presbyterian congregation, in the Northern Liberties."

After prayer, and a free conversation on the subject named, this little company organized themselves into what they denominated an "Association," having for its object the "purchase of a lot of ground, and the erection thereon of a building of sufficient dimensions to accommodate a congregation, and also to be so constructed as to be useful for Sunday and infant schools, and any other object by which the morals and minds of the youth of this neighborhood may be improved."

Frequent meetings of the Association were held, and arrangements were soon entered into to purchase ground on the north side of Coates street, below Fourth. At this place there were two lots adjoining, belonging to different owners, and occupied at the time with small houses. To one of these owners was given $4,000, and to the other $3,650, making a total for the lots and buildings thereon of $7,650.

The Association added other persons to their mem-

"THE OLD CHURCH"

bership, and they held the property, which they secured, in stock, at $200 per share.

The two lots purchased, when thrown into one, had a frontage on Coates street of 80 feet, and ran back to a depth of 157 feet.

The work of cleaning the ground, and preparing for building, was soon actively commenced. The small houses on the front of the lot, to the east and west, were allowed to remain, while an avenue, 30 feet wide, was opened in the center, running back 81 feet from the building line on Coates street. Where this avenue ended, the front of the church building stood.

The building itself was 61 feet wide by 66 feet deep. It was built of stone and rough-cast. Its design was plain, but attractive, and was in rigid conformity to the style of church architecture common at that day.

The trees which grew on either side of the long avenue, gave a special attractiveness to the exterior as one approached the building, and we have no doubt that its projectors and builders regarded it *complete*, as completeness was reckoned in those days. When finished, it had on the main floor of the audience-room one hundred and seventeen pews, and in the gallery thirty pews. These pews afforded sitting accommodation for about seven hundred persons.

On the lower floor, there were the lecture room, which was used also as the main Sunday School room; the session and trustees' room, and the Infant Sunday School room.

Like all the lecture rooms of churches built about this time, the one in this church was, in the true sense of that word, a *basement*. Its floor was several feet below the line of the pavement, and we wonder not, that in our day, many complaints were made of its darkness and dampness.

One of the essentials of a church property in those days, was to have provision made for the burial of the dead. Hence, burial vaults were arranged on the east side, and in front of the building. Some of these were designed for the poor of the church, some for rent to outside parties, and some for sale to any desiring to purchase.

The work of building had so far progressed during the spring and summer of 1835, that on the 12th of October, the Association appointed a committee to invite the congregation worshiping in Commissioners' Hall, which had been duly organized as the Central Presbyterian Church in the Northern Liberties, to come, with their pastor, and hold their services in the Session room of the new building.

This invitation was accepted, and on the 14th of November, 1835, this church and congregation, not only met there for worship, but with appropriate exercises formally dedicated the lower room to the service of God.*

* A short time before the opening of the church, the pastor had ruptured a blood vessel. In a very weak condition, he attended the opening services. Rev. Mr. Bacon, a city missionary, preached the sermon. The pastor offered the prayer, and baptized Miss Malvina Walton, who was received into the church on profession of faith. This was the last time Mr. Burroughs was in the church.

While the work of finishing the main room of the building was going on, the attention of the congregation was directed to the framing of a Constitution, and the securing of a Charter.

A Constitution was adopted in the beginning of the year 1836, and the Charter was obtained and recorded at Harrisburg, July 8th, of the same year.

Under this Constitution and Charter the following persons constituted the first Board of Trustees:

BENJAMIN NAGLEE, CHARLES ELLIOT, JOHN A. STEWART,	To serve until the second Monday in January, 1837.
EDWARD PATTESON, CASPAR YEAGER, PETER MINTZER,	To serve until the second Monday in January, 1838.
JOSEPH POND, JOSEPH NAGLEE, JOHN G. FLEGEL,	To serve until the second Monday in January, 1839.

The first annual meeting of the congregation, under the Charter, was held January 9th, 1837; at which time Messers. B. Naglee, C. Elliot, and J. A. Stewart, whose term of service in the Board had expired, were *elected by ballot*, to serve for three years.

The first meeting of the Board of Trustees, under the Charter, was held July 27th, 1836. An election for officers took place with the following result:

President, CHARLES ELLIOT.
Secretary, EDWARD PATTESON.
Treasurer, BENJAMIN NAGLEE.

At this meeting a committee was appointed to confer with the Association, relative to the transfer of their property to this congregation. Also, a committee to draft suitable By-Laws for the government of the Board.

While these temporal interests were being considered, the church was not neglecting spiritual affairs. They maintained their services regularly, and the spirit of the records shows that all the members were awake to do the "will of God."

Their pastor, however, Rev. Wm. H. Burroughs, was compelled by feeble health to leave them, and in less than one year from the time of his installation, God called him "Home."

There were added to the church, during his ministry, twenty-three persons.

CALL DECLINED.

The congregation met, agreeably to notice given from the pulpit, on Tuesday evening, May 10th, 1836, to proceed if the way be clear, to the election of a pastor. At this meeting they elected Rev. Robert Dunlap, then of Danville, as their pastor, Mr. Dunlap, however, declined to accept the call of this congregation.

III.

REV. T. A. J. MINES, THE SECOND PASTOR.

About the 1st of August, 1836, the upper part of the church building was finished and appropriately opened for Divine Service.

The people, who had (since the dissolution of Mr. Burroughs' pastoral relation) been depending on supplies for their pulpit, now took steps to call a pastor.

Accordingly, on the 26th of August, 1836, a congregational meeting was held, and Rev. Thomas A. J. Mines was elected pastor. He was installed in the month of September following. His ministry among the people was brief. Sickness compelled him, at the end of two months, to retire from the work.*

The congregation were again dependent on pulpit supplies, but the people kept in good heart, and diligently applied themselves to their labors.

The committee of the Trustees appointed to confer with the Association relative to the transfer of their property to the congregation, made their report August 13th, 1836. It was in substance as follows:

"The Association express a willingness to transfer

---

* We have been unable to obtain detailed information concerning Mr. Mines. We know only that he was born in Virginia, and that in 1832 he was received as a student in the Theological Seminary at Princeton, N. J. Here he continued for a little over a year, when he went to Maysville, Ky.; then to Germantown, Pa.; and afterwards to Carbondale, Pa. He was preaching at the latter place when he received the call to this church, which he accepted. This was his last charge. Upon resigning, he went to the house of his father, Rev. John Mines, who then lived at Rockville, Md. After an illness of about fifteen months, God called him home.

the property now held by them in Coates street, near Fourth, to this congregation, provided this congregation pay them the amount of money advanced by them, and assume all the responsibility incurred by them in purchasing the lot, and erecting the building and burial vaults, so as to release them."

This proposition was accepted by the Trustees, and a committee was appointed to make the arrangements and receive the transfer, subject to the approval of the congregation.

Considerable delay occurred before the matter was consummated; a delay, as we learn from the report of the Trustees, made at a congregational meeting held January 8th, 1838, occasioned by the unfinished condition of the church, and the unfinished state of the accounts of the Association.

At this meeting the congregation empowered the Board of Trustees to make all the necessary arrangements for the transfer of the property to them, and to call the congregation together when they were ready to report.

At a meeting of the congregation, held April 24th, 1838, the terms of the transfer were read in detail, and, on motion, "the Trustees were authorized to carry the conditions of the Association into effect, by giving corporation notes, and executing the deeds and mortgages therein specified."

The whole cost of the property, including lot, building and vaults, was $23,433.85. Deducting the amount credited to the congregation from the time

A. Reed

of its occupancy of the building, there was a balance still due the Association of $21,289.92. This was the actual indebtedness of the church at the time of the transfer. From the sale of pews and burial vaults, this amount was afterwards reduced to $17,039.92, which was called the "standing debt."

The congregation, at the time they accepted the property, with the heavy debt resting upon it, was comparatively small. The records show quite clearly that the average attendance upon the Sabbath services was less than two hundred persons. Yet they were a people accustomed to church hardships and church toil; and, as their annual reports in these early years so frequently express it, they labored patiently, zealously and unitedly, trusting ever in the blessing of God.

IV.

REV. ANSON ROOD, THE THIRD PASTOR.*

It was the good fortune of this people, under God, to call as their pastor Rev. Anson Rood, from Danbury, Connecticut. He was duly installed December 15th, 1837. His salary was fixed at $1000 per annum. It seems that Mr. Rood was eminently qualified

* Mr. Rood was born in Vermont. He graduated at Middleburg College, Vt., in 1825. For a short time after graduation he was a student in Princeton Theological Seminary. He was ordained a pastor of the church at Danbury, Conn., April 23d, 1829. He continued with his first charge until he accepted the call to this church. After resigning his pastoral charge of this church, his health never permitted him to undertake the work again.

to encourage the people. He entered heartily into their work. He was one with them.

We might reasonably expect that there would be embarrassing times for years to come, after a feeble church had assumed such a weight of debt. But it was comforting to this people to have in their pastor one who, never despairing, bade them "go forward."

While it is bewildering to us to read of liabilities, deficiencies, loans and mortgages, which constantly meet our eyes in turning the pages of our earliest records, it is quite gratifying to discover that those who have gone before us were never slow to suggest ways and means to meet the demands upon them.

The pastor constantly stirred up the people, from the pulpit, to a remembrance that these must be met. Subscription papers were started on the Sabbath, and during the week. These were scarcely out of sight before others were presented. Such rooms as could be used were rented for week-day schools. The ladies formed a "Mite Society." The people were earnestly solicited to give more liberally to the Sabbath collections. All the income of the church was voted to meet the claims upon it, and the pastor's salary was to be met by voluntary subscriptions. Pew rents were raised, and lowered, and raised again, as the exigency of the case required. Money was raised on mortgage, so that a previous mortgage might be paid, and those who had it in their power frequently relieved the church from pressing claims, by making temporary loans.

Such was, in brief, the condition of temporal things during the nine years succeeding the time of the transfer of the property from the Association to the congregation.

During the spring of 1847, a determined effort began to change the aspect of affairs. A committee, in conjunction with the pastor, undertook to raise an amount sufficient to free the church from all embarrassment. They were so far successful that on May 26th, 1847, according to a previous announcement, the congregation met to congratulate each other, and return thanks to God. At this meeting a series of congratulatory resolutions were adopted; and after enjoying some refreshments, which had been provided, the congregation adjourned.

The measure of this success, as we find reported at a congregational meeting, held January 11th, 1848, was the reduction of the "permanent debt" from $15,200 to $8,750. During that same year the two lots on Coates street, to the front of and east and west of the church, and running back eighty feet, were sold to parties with the understanding that they should erect thereon two fine brick dwellings. For these lots the Board of Trustees received $3,000. This amount with the special effort before named, enabled the Trustees, in their annual report, presented in 1848, to announce the "permanent debt" of the church to be $5,750. In addition to this, they reported also a floating debt of $1,349.

During these years, when the congregation was

struggling to maintain itself, we do well to remember that it was not forgetful of the wants of others. The church was opened time and again for worthy objects. The Tract, the Bible, the Mission, and other causes, were allowed to be presented, and appeals for help were cheerfully and liberally responded to. So truly was this the case, and so generally was the fact known, that our church had the honorable reputation of being one of the most benevolent in the city. So deeply interested was the pastor in behalf of the needy, that his seeking after them, and making provision for their necessities, amounted almost to a passion. He not only cheerfully gave of his own substance, but canvassed his congregation for further gifts, to help the deserving poor whom he had previously sought out. His large-heartedness was fully understood and appreciated by the congregation. They in turn sought to "devise liberal things." They kept their property in good repair, altered it, sometimes at considerable expense, if the improvements of the times or the comforts of the people required it.

For the first time in its history, the building was closed from the latter part of June, 1841, until the 8th of August, for repairs. During this time it was thoroughly cleaned and painted. An organ was placed in the gallery, pipes were introduced into the building, and gaslight took the place of oil light. In every way the people sought to make the place suitable for a worshiping assembly.

It is not to be wondered at that God gave spiritual blessings to those who were bent upon building up his church. He continually reminded them that he was with them. During these years he poured out his Holy Spirit, and there were added unto the church a goodly number of souls.

One precious revival began in the winter of 1842, and continued without interruption for twelve weeks. It was denominated "The Great Revival." Meetings were held every evening but Saturday evening, and, as a result, more than one hundred were converted, and added to the church.

Mr. Rood's health had become greatly impaired, so that he was compelled to seek rest from his pastoral cares. Accordingly he addressed the following letter to the Session of the church, and they, in turn, laid it before the people at a congregational meeting held January 24th, 1849.

Dear Brethren:

I address you, as the proper organ of communication with the church and congregation, in reference to a subject mutually interesting to them and myself. For many weeks as is well known, I have been laid aside from my usual labors, and I see no prospect of being able to resume them. I am quite sensible that the congregation whose interests I have had so much at heart, must suffer inconvenience and injury by this long suspension of pastoral labor; and I have resolved, therefore, to resign my pastoral charge, that there may be no impediment in filling my place with one whose time and energies, shall be devoted to the work in which I have been engaged. In taking this step (which it is proper to say is entirely the prompting of my own convictions of duty), there are a thousand tender recollections, and associations, which press upon my mind. I think of months and years that are past, of the harmonies and happy charge I left to come among you; of my hopes and plans, my desires and aims. But on this topic, I must not, I cannot dwell. In my present circumstances as may well be supposed, an enlargement upon them must be extremely painful to me.

Let me through you, express to all the members of the church and congregation, my sincere thanks for all their kind attention and regard. We have lived together in great harmony. We shall part, I am sure, with feelings of mutual kindness and good will. That the richest blessings of the Good Shepherd, may rest on you and yours, that you may be firmly established in the faith, and devoted to every good word and work, is the desire and prayer of your sincere friend and pastor,

(Signed) A. Rood.

PHILADELPHIA, January 6, 1849.

After the reading of the letter from Mr. Rood, a committee, consisting of Messrs. E. D. Tarr, R. M. Foust, Wm. Sanderson, and Isaac Ashmead, was appointed to draft resolutions, expressive of the sentiments of the meeting. The congregation engaged in devotional exercises, until the committee were prepared to report.

After a season of absence, the majority of the committee reported as follows:

Resolved, 1st. That, in view of the peculiar state of the Rev. A. Rood's health, and his consequent desire to withdraw from the pastoral duties of this church and congregation; we do not deem it advisable to oppose his expressed desire to be dismissed.

Resolved, 2d. That this congregation deeply and sincerely regret, that the health of Mr. Rood, was deemed by him such as to make it necessary, in his opinion, to withdraw from his pastoral relations with this church.

Resolved, 3d. That the uniform and consistent character, the amiable and Christian deportment, the zealous and untiring and successful discharge of the pastoral relations of the Rev. A. Rood, call forth our highest admiration and commendation, and cause us to feel more sensibly the pangs of separation.

Resolved, 4th. That, in retiring from the position in which for a long season he has faithfully labored, our pastor carries with him our regret for the separation, our sympathies for his trials, and our earnest prayers for his speedy recovery to health.

Resolved, 5th. That three members of this congregation be appointed to represent this congregation in Presbytery.

Mr. Isaac Ashmead, the other member of the committee, who had not subscribed to the resolutions as offered, proposed the following as an amendment: To strike out all after the first word, "Resolved," and insert the following: "That in view of the peculiar circumstances in which our pastor has been for a long time placed, it is inexpedient to take action upon his communication at the present time."

The people, by the discussion which followed, gave

evidence that they were not yet prepared to act in the matter. They disposed of the whole subject at that meeting, by laying the communication from their pastor, with the resolutions of their committee, and the proposed amendment, upon the table, and adjourned to meet March 5th, 1849.

At this meeting, the following preamble and resolution were adopted unanimously:

"WHEREAS, The session communicates the fact to the meeting this evening, that the Rev. A. Rood, in a letter dated February 23d, 1849, has renewed his desire that his resignation should be accepted; therefore,

Resolved, That the resolutions reported at the meeting held January 24th, be adopted.

Messrs. Elihu D. Tarr, Robert M. Foust, and Geo. C. Bower, were appointed commissioners to represent the church and congregation at the next meeting of the Presbytery.

Messrs. B. D. Stewart, Wm. Sanderson, Thos. Beaver, Saml. T. Bodine, and Henry Davis, were appointed a committee to wait upon Rev. A. Rood, and communicate to him the proceedings of this meeting.

From this time Mr. Rood was unable to resume the pastoral work. As much as lay in his power, however, he tried to work for his Master. The people of this church continued to hold him in affectionate remembrance, and their regard for him was embodied in the following preamble and resolutions, which are recorded in the minutes of Session February 22d, 1858:

WHEREAS, The Rev. Anson Rood departed this life November 27th, 1857; and

WHEREAS, from December 15th, 1837, to March 5th, 1849, Mr. Rood was the beloved pastor of the Central Presbyterian Church, N. L.; and

WHEREAS, we consider it alike the duty and the privilege of the Church of Christ to glorify God in those who have been faithful unto death; therefore,

Resolved, That in our deceased friend and pastor we recognize one who, with no ordinary zeal and self-denial, faithfully served his day and generation, aiming, to the full extent of his powers, alike by the pulpit and the press, to promote the welfare of the cause of Christ, of his country, and the world.

Resolved, That during the time that he went out and in among us as our pastor, there is but one testimony to be given by us to his love for souls, his zeal for the honor of Christ, his sympathy with the destitute and the ignorant, and his steadfast imitation of the example of Him who went about doing good. Foremost in every good word and work, whether of a local or a general character, eminently sagacious, far-seeing and public-spirited, his meat and his drink it was to do the will of his Father in heaven.

Resolved, That while we thus bear our cordial and united testimony as to his official character, we also remember him as the honest and upright man, the warm-hearted and sincere friend. The sympathy and respect already manifested for him by his brethren in the ministry, we fully respond to and reciprocate, as the people of his charge.

During the eleven years and three months that Mr. Rood was pastor of this church, there were added to the membership four hundred and thirty persons.

REV. T. J. SHEPHERD, DECLINES A CALL.

About three months after the resignation of Mr. Rood, the people, believing that they had heard a sufficient number of candidates preach in their pulpit, united in a request to the Session, to call a congregational meeting, for the purpose, if the way be clear, of electing a pastor.

The Session acceded to this request, and accordingly a meeting of the congregation was held June 8th, 1849. At this meeting the Rev. T. J. Shepherd was elected pastor. Mr. Shepherd at that time was pastor of the Harmony Presbyterian Church, Lisbon, Md., and a member of the Presbytery of the District of Columbia. At the present time he is the pastor of the First Presbyterian Church, N. L.

Messrs. R. M. Foust, E. D. Tarr and S. T. Bodine were appointed commissioners, on the part of the congregation, to prosecute the call before the Presbytery of the District of Columbia. This Committee met the last-named Presbytery in the city of Washington, August 7th, 1849. They pressed the claims of this congregation before that body, when, by a majority of *one* in Presbytery, the call was put into the hands of Mr. Shepherd. He declined to accept it, giving his reasons before his co-presbyters. These reasons he afterwards embodied in a letter, which was read at a meeting of this congregation, held August 31st, 1849. From this letter we learn that the peculiar necessities of the charge he then had, the interests which he had excited, and which

James P. Wilson

needed his further encouragement; the transition state of his church from a missionary to a self-sustaining condition; the divided sentiment among his brethren in Presbytery on the subject of his removal, together with other reasons, had determined him in his decision.

Many hopes had been cherished by this people that the acceptance of their call by Mr. Shepherd would greatly advance the interests of the church. These hopes were destroyed for a time by his declination.

V.

REV. JAMES P. WILSON, D.D., THE FOURTH PASTOR.*

The congregation had now been without a pastor for ten months. I cannot better express the state of things at that time than by collating the language of others, as found in the Minute Book.

---

* Dr. Wilson was born in Philadelphia, Pa. He was ready for college when he was twelve years old, but did not enter until he was thirteen, and graduated at the University of Pennsylvania when he was sixteen years of age. He engaged in teaching, first at Hartsville, and then at Lancaster, Pa. In the spring of 1829 he commenced his theological studies under his father, Rev. James P. Wilson, D.D., who was said to be one of the best preachers in this country. He was licensed to preach by the Philadelphia Presbytery October 20th, 1830, and in 1839 was ordained and installed pastor of the church in Neshaminy. In July, 1847, he was elected President of Delaware College, Newark, Del.; and in March, 1850, was installed as the pastor of this church. In the fall of 1850 he accepted the Professorship of Systematic Theology in Union Theological Seminary, N. Y., and in the fall of 1853 resigned his Professorship, and was installed as pastor of a new church in Newark, N. J., where he still continues.

"The congregation had become discouraged and scattered. The church edifice needed not only remodeling, but repairing within and without."

"Money, greatly needed, was not possessed, and with difficulty could hardly be obtained."

"The members were comparatively few, and these, by reason of frequent disappointments, and the hopeless aspect of affairs, had lost much of their former fervor and zeal."

At this juncture the congregation (Jan. 4th, 1850) called Rev. James P. Wilson, D.D., to become their pastor. He was at that time President of Delaware College, at Newark, Delaware. Being a man of commanding talents and elevated piety, it was believed that, under God, he would save the church and add largely to its power.

The acceptance of the call by Dr. Wilson infused a new life among the people. They remodeled the interior of the church building. They had it re-painted and re-papered, and several pledged themselves to make up all deficiencies. The promised salary of Dr. Wilson was $1,500 per annum, but the revenue from pews enabled the congregation, at an adjourned meeting, held February 24th, 1851, to vote an increase to $2,000.

Everything was promising well, when the congregation was unexpectedly disturbed with rumors that their pastor was called to a neighboring city. These rumors quickly were resolved into shape, for it became known that Dr. Wilson had been elected to the chair of Theology in Union Theological Seminary, New York City.

At a meeting of the congregation, held January 13th, 1851, Messrs. E. D. Tarr, B. D. Stewart, W. F. Smith, R. M. Foust, S. T. Bodine, C. Moore, and J. A. Spencer, were appointed a committee to draft resolutions expressive of the views of the congregation regarding this matter. These resolutions are embodied in the report of the commissioners afterwards chosen to represent the church in Presbytery.

The Fourth Presbytery of Philadelphia cited the congregation to appear, by their commissioners, at a meeting to be held in the church, on Tuesday, February 18th, 1851, to show cause why their pastor should not be translated to another field of labor.

In accordance with this citation, the congregation, at a meeting held February 13th, 1851, appointed Messrs. H. H. Shillingford, E. D. Tarr, S. T. Bodine, R. M. Foust, and Henry Davis, commissioners, with instructions to oppose, by all suitable and Christian means, such translation.

The work of these commissioners will be best understood by giving in full their report as made to the congregation, February 24th, 1851:

"*To the Members of the Church and Congregation of the Central Presbyterian Church in the Northern Liberties.*

"BRETHREN:—The undersigned, commissioners appointed to represent this corporation in the Fourth Presbytery of Philadelphia, at a meeting of that body, held in this place on the 18th inst., to take into consideration the application of the Union Theological Seminary of New York, for the services of our pastor, who had been elected to the Professorship of Theology in that institution, report:

"That they have attended to the duties of their appointment, and are now prepared to make report of their proceedings in detail, and surrender up to this body the powers thus delegated to them.

"It must be perfectly understood by all that the claims for the services of Dr. J. P. Wilson for this Seminary, if admitted, involved the loss of our pastor. The question, therefore, was one of the greatest interest to this church, and so the commissioners felt it. And perhaps it was well that it was so, for the magnitude of the subject inspired their zeal, and nerved them for the effort; and, by the grace of God, they are happy to say that their efforts have been blessed and crowned with success.

"The commissioners deemed it most advisable to place upon paper the views entertained by them, and, as they believed, by this congregation, and give a consecutive history of the church and its operations from the time of the call of Dr. Wilson to the present time. This they believed would greatly facilitate the prosecution of the matter by the members of the Presbytery, in the understanding of the subject, and appreciating the opposition to the removal of Dr. Wilson, and such they believe was the effect of that statement.

"Another object had in view was, that their action, whether for good or evil, could be reported to and reviewed by you. That paper, with all its imperfections, was submitted to the Presbytery after much prayer, and with great anxiety as to your sentiments upon this important matter. It is as follows:

To the Members of the Fourth Presbytery of Philadelphia.

"BRETHREN:—The undersigned have been appointed commissioners to your body from the Central Presbyterian Church, N. L., as will appear from the action of the church and congregation, now before you, in obedience to a citation from you, in regard to the subject of the dismissal of the Rev. James P. Wilson, D.D., the present pastor of said church. They therefore deem it expedient to present for your consideration the following statement of facts and views, so that should the Presbytery decide in favor of removing him from his present charge, the fearful responsibility may rest with them, under a full knowledge of the facts in the case.

"In January, 1850, this church had been without a stated minister for upwards of ten months. The congregation had become discouraged and scattered. The church edifice was greatly out of repair, and needed much, a modernizing hand. To make the necessary alterations and repairs, a considerable amount of funds were required, and a great rallying point made necessary; for our finances were exhausted, our resources cut off, our members comparatively few, and of these the love of many waxed faint, and others became entirely discouraged.

"At this juncture, it was deemed, by those members of the church whose faith took a firm hold upon the blessed promises revealed in God's word, to be their duty to make a united and persevering effort to procure the services of one whose commanding talents and elevated piety would not only secure this church from impending ruin, but place "Constitutional Presbyterianism"* in this section of the city on a firm basis.

"Thus believing, and thus aiming, under the lead of Divine Providence, they made selection of the Rev. J. P. Wilson, D.D., and unanimously elected him their pastor. To insure his services, it became necessary that the church edifice should be altered and repaired, involving a cost of upwards of $2,300, and that provision should be made for an increase of salary after the first year. This was promptly done, and a few individuals pledged themselves to the congregation that they would see the matter fairly through, and make up any deficiency in the current expenses of the church. With this understanding, the call was made out and accepted.

"This understanding cost those who pledged themselves for the deficiency the sum rising $2,200, but they faithfully kept their engagement; and as the

* A title designating the former "New School" branch of the church.

end of the fiscal year approached they congratulated themselves upon the bright prospects which gilded the future. They saw, with pleasure and deep gratitude an increasing congregation, a growing interest on the subject of our holy religion, and every indication to inspire the belief that the day was not far distant when enough could be spared to plant a branch from this vine in the adjoining and flourishing district of Spring Garden, where but one "Constitutional" church now exists—the Logan Square Church.

"Just at this critical moment came the call from the New York Theological Seminary, for the services of Dr. Wilson, the effect of which, with all the other painful circumstances, has been to distract our people, paralyze our efforts, and threaten the dearest interests of this branch of the Presbyterian Church in this section of the city.

"We cannot but look upon this call as exceedingly untimely and unfortunate, when viewed in connection with some of the means used in prosecuting it. After carefully weighing all the arguments and reasons presented by our brethren, the committee from the Seminary, we cannot bring our minds to the conclusion that the call should be responded to. We have looked in vain for the evidence to justify us in such a belief. On the contrary, all the indications of God's overruling Providence in the matter are, to our own hearts and minds, conclusive that this is the field of labor to which our beloved pastor is called. It is true that twenty out of thirty of the Trustees of the Seminary joined in the call, and forwarded it through a very able and zealous committee,* who, as we think, have pressed the claims of the Seminary with undue ardor. As illustrative of this point, we state that this committee have, as they themselves say, visited this city some five different times previous to this, to press this call upon our pastor, without the knowledge of the authorities of the church and congregation; in addition to which, the following announcement appeared in the New York *Tribune* on the 12th inst.:

"UNION THEOLOGICAL SEMINARY.—Rev. Henry B. Smith will be inaugurated as Professor of Ecclesiastical History in this institution, at the Mercer Street Church, this evening. Prof. Smith will deliver an address and the charge will be delivered by Rev. Dr. Cox. The services will commence at 7½ o'clock. Rev. James P. Wilson, D.D., has signified to the Fourth Presbytery of Philadelphia, of which he is a member, his conviction that it is his duty to accept the call from the Seminary to be Professor of Theology. On the accession of Dr. Wilson the Faculty will be complete. It is expected that he will enter upon his new labors as soon as he can regularly be transferred to the institution."

"This announcement was followed by one of a similar, but more conclusive character, by Rev. Samuel H. Cox, D.D., one of the committee, from the pulpit of the church, and at the meeting referred to in the

* Drs Cox and Skinner.

above notice. In the *New York Observer* of the 13th inst. the following notice appeared:

"UNION THEOLOGICAL SEMINARY.—Rev. James P. Wilson, D.D., has signified to the Fourth Presbytery of Philadelphia, of which he is a member, his conviction that it is his duty to accept the call from the Union Theological Seminary of this city, to be Professor of Theology in that institution. It is understood that neither the Presbytery nor his church, strongly attached as they are to their pastor, intends to make opposition to his coming. On the accession of Dr. Wilson, the Faculty will be complete. It is expected that he will soon enter upon his new labors."

"The effect of these announcements on the public mind may be gathered from the following editorial in the *North American*, of this city, on the morning of the 13th inst.:

"The Rev. James P. Wilson, D.D., who has for some time past had charge of a congregation in this city, has accepted a call to become Professor of Theology in the Union Theological Seminary of New York."

"It will be borne in mind that this editorial followed the announcement made in the *Tribune*, and at the Mercer Street Church, in the evening of the same day, and came out in the morning of the day when our congregational meeting took place in the evening. This was so far from a correct statement of the fact, that Dr. Wilson deemed it but proper and just to authorize the following contradiction.

which appeared in the *North American*, of this city, on the 14th inst.:

"The Rev. James P. Wilson, of whom we yesterday announced, on the authority of a New York paper, that he had accepted the Professorship of Theology in the Union Theological Seminary of that city, informs us that he has not yet responded to the invitation."

"It would scarcely be prudent for the commissioners to say that there was any design in the foregoing announcement to forestall public sentiment, or influence the action of this body. We simply state the facts, and leave the conclusions to be drawn by the Presbytery.

"The recent settlement of Dr. Wilson among us, under the circumstances named; the great necessity for his valuable labors in this section; the wide field of usefulness here opened, and the great jeopardy in which it would place the interests of our congregation and Constitutional Presbyterianism, as before remarked, would, to our minds, indicate anything but reasons in favor of his removal at this time.

"In this connection, it seems but proper to state that the location of our church, occupying as it does a central position in what may be deemed the city of Philadelphia, and in the midst of a population of one hundred thousand, and where our connection has but two congregations, is a matter not to be overlooked in the decision of this question. Dr. Wilson and his congregation are happy in the connection, and neither of them urge, or in fact ask its severance, except the former, as a matter of form, to secure the opinion and counsel of this Presbytery. This is seen by the action of the congregation at their regular annual meeting, January 13th, which we here annex, and the statement of the views of Dr. Wilson, as made at the congregational meeting on the 13th inst., which is also annexed:

RESOLUTIONS OF THE CONGREGATION.

Resolved, 1st. That this people have heard, with unfeigned regret, of the efforts which are being made in a sister city to take from us our beloved pastor, and to transfer his valuable labors from this to a distant field.

Resolved, 2d. That, in our opinion, such change seems fraught with danger to the best interests of this church and the cause of Constitutional Presbyterianism in this community, it being well known and understood that this portion of the vineyard was the ground on which was fought the battle for the supremacy of the principles we so dearly love and cherish.

Resolved, 3d. That the eminent abilities and endearing manners of our pastor, Rev. James P. Wilson, D.D., have engaged our esteem and love, and ensured his future usefulness amongst us and our children. That his present field of labor is extensive and increasing, involving the interests of a widespread and growing neighborhood, in which we earnestly believe the influence of this church is destined to operate favorably in the highest degree.

Resolved, 4th. That, in view of all the circumstances, the attachment of this people to their pastor, the prospective ultimate good which may reasonably be anticipated from his labors amongst us; the certain injury which will accrue to the interests of this church and congregation if he leave us—all induce an earnest expression of the hope that he will (God giving him wisdom so as best to decide) consent to remain with us, and allow our present pastoral relations to remain undisturbed.

Resolved, 5th. That a copy of these resolutions be sent to our pastor, signed by the President and Secretary of the meeting.

STATEMENT OF DR. WILSON'S VIEWS, AT THE CONGREGATIONAL MEETING ON THE 13TH INST.:

"The paper which I gave to the New York committee expressed my views entirely, and I still adhere to the views therein expressed. Still I consider the question entirely open for the decision of the Presbytery, to whom I refer the whole subject; and if they shall decide against my going, I will cheerfully submit to their decision, and shall, in submitting to their judgment, conclude that my views of duty in this respect were not well founded, and shall expect to feel perfectly happy in staying where I now am, and experience no longing desire to go to New York. I have no private reasons to influence me in my views of duty. My present relation is all that I could desire. My people are kind and united, and if I studied my own ease and personal comfort alone, I should decide to stay; as I believe the duties of the station to which I am called would be far more laborious, and I would necessarily have less sympathy in their discharge than in my present situation. This I should feel, as I have been accustomed to have the sympathy of a congregation.

"I wish it to be distinctly understood that I have not decided to go. And if any one has made such an assertion, he has done it without my authority, and upon his own responsibility. Nor have I decided to stay. And if any one has so asserted, it was unauthorized by me. I shall be governed by the action of Presbytery, and surrender my views of duty to their judgment.

"Should the Presbytery refuse to decide the question, or throw it back for my decision, I shall conceive it my duty to go. Should they decide in favor of my dismissal, I shall go; but should they decide against my dismissal, I shall not go, and shall, as I said before, be perfectly cheerful and happy in an acquiescence in their decision."

"It is due to Dr. Wilson, and proper to state, that the above views were given orally at the meeting, and written out by the commissioners, as they recollected and understood them, and are believed to be substantially correct.

"The following is the paper which was in the hands of and read by Dr. Wilson himself, at the former meeting of this body, in this place, and referred to by him in his statement to the congregation on the 13th inst.:

"This call has been before my mind for several weeks. I have considered it *in extenso*, on all sides, and religiously, with a sincere desire, as far as I know myself, to ascertain and do the will of God. My present impressions are, on the whole, favorable to the idea that it is my duty to accept it; and unless some moral obstacle shall arise, not now anticipated, either from the Presbytery or from my congregation, both of whom I kindly and deeply consider in the question, I shall probably see it my duty to respond to said call an answer in the affirmative. And unless Presbytery interpose some obstacle of the above sort, it now seems my duty so to respond to it."

"It will be seen by the statement of Dr. Wilson's views, that the question is entirely open for the action of Presbytery, and they must meet it. A refusal on their part to act, is a virtual decision in favor of his dismissal, as in that case he expressly says he shall conceive it his duty to go. But if they decide it not to be his duty to accept the invitation, he will cheerfully acquiesce in their opinion and remain. So the question must be fairly met by this body, and we trust it will be so met, and promptly decided.

"We have now made a plain and unvarnished statement of facts, and if the Presbytery can, under all the circumstances of the case, sever a connection so happy in all points of view, but so fraught with evil if broken up, theirs must be the responsibility; and we shall have the abiding consolation, in all after time, in the review, that we did what we could to avert the direful consequences should they follow.

H. H. SHILLINGFORD,
ELIHU D. TARR,
ROBERT M. FOUST,
SAMUEL T. BODINE,
HENRY DAVIS,
} *Commissioners.*

FEBRUARY 15, 1851.

The Presbytery having heard all the parties in the case, refused to dismiss Dr. Wilson. This action gave very great and general satisfaction to the church.

A few weeks after this, Dr. Wilson addressed a letter to the Session and Board of Trustees of the church, expressing his conviction that he ought to accept the call to New York.

A congregational meeting was called on April 1st, 1851, when the letter was read, and is as follows:

Philadelphia, March 12, 1851.

DEAR BRETHREN:—I received a communication on the first of this month, informing me of the formal reiterations of the call of the Directors of the New York Theological Seminary, which was issued by the Fourth Presbytery at their meeting on the 18th ult.

This second urgent invitation, so soon after the rejection of the first, and with equal unanimity, seems to leave me no longer any alternative but to accept at once, and ask you to unite with me in a request to the congregation for their consent to a dissolution of the pastoral relation.

My convictions of duty from the first have been plain and clear. The only difficulty in the way has been the probable injury of the congregation, and considerations of their welfare, and the general interests of religion, and of the church in this community.

Impressed, and almost overwhelmed, with these considerations, and deeply affected with the constant manifestations of the kindness and affectionate attachment of the people of my charge, I long hesitated and strove against my convictions, and felt that I could not make up my mind to break away and sunder a tie so recently formed.

I wished to consult the feelings of my brethren in the Presbytery, and felt willing to submit my convictions to their united judgment, and let the matter rest ultimately on their decision. A meeting of the Presbytery was accordingly held, and a result obtained. I cheerfully acquiesced in this issue, although, from the whole discussion before the Presbytery, my previous convictions were only deepened as to the path which Providence seemed clearly to point out. I felt, however, entirely satisfied, and sincerely hoped that the protracted difficulty was at an end.

But the call is now repeated with increased earnestness, and comes to me with the power and claim of a direct summons from the Head of the Church, and I know not how to resist it any longer. I now feel that I must go, and I ask you to resist no more, but cheerfully, and with faith in God, resign your opposition, and unite with me in acting according to my clear convictions of duty.

I am truly thankful that, from the nature and cir-circumstances of the post which I am solicited to accept, there is no possibility of any motive interfering to lead my mind to an improper decision.

Were I to consult my interest, both in regard to pecuniary matters, or personal ease and comfort, I should remain where I am. There is no temptation, therefore, for me to deceive myself, or impose on my own judgment in coming to a right decision.

If I know myself, in this whole transaction, my single and only aim has been to do my duty to God, and to obey my conscience. I must ask you, then, to let me go.

I repeat, what I have always said, and must ever say, that no one could be more pleasantly situated in any field of labor, or meet with more facilities and encouragements, and warm-hearted co-operation, in the performance of his work, amongst any people, than I have experienced amongst you. Your kindness and affection has been constant, and far better than I have deserved; and nothing less than a conviction of responsibility, that I cannot resist or evade, compels me to come before you and ask your acquiescence in my request for a dissolution of the pastoral relation.

May God guide and direct your judgment, and give you faith to acquiesce in what seems to be evident indications of his will.

(Signed) JAMES P. WILSON, *Pastor.*

After the reading of this letter, the congregation adopted the following preamble and resolutions:

WHEREAS, a communication has been presented by the Session, from our pastor, Rev. J. P. Wilson, D.D., in which he states that the call from New York Theological Seminary has been renewed, and is pressed with renewed zeal, and that he feels it to be his duty, and it is his intention, to accept the call, and asks us to unite with him in the application to Presbytery, for a dissolution of the present relations; therefore,

Resolved, 1st. That we have looked in vain for any new light upon this subject, calculated to change the views we held, and presented to Presbytery at a former meeting. We think the case stands now precisely as it stood then; for, if we are correctly informed, there has not even been a new election by the Trustees of the Seminary; and we must be permitted to say, that we feel no little surprise and sorrow that this question should be so soon again agitated; for we feel that the action of Presbytery, already had upon this subject, was to be considered a final settlement of the question. And so believing, this congregation have laid their plans accordingly, and with the intention of promoting both the usefulness and comfort of our pastor.

Resolved, 2d. That as we have never desired a separation, we cannot, therefore, unite with our pastor in an application to Presbytery for a dissolution of the pastoral relation now existing.

Resolved, 3d. That as Dr. Wilson has made up his mind to insist upon a dissolution of his pastoral relations with this church, we deem it inexpedient to oppose his wishes.

Resolved, 4th. That the elder who may represent this church in meeting of Presbytery, be requested to present the foregoing resolutions and statement to Presbytery.

The application of Dr. Wilson for a dissolution of his pastoral relation to this church, was renewed at the spring meeting of Presbytery, held April 8th, 1851, when it was granted. The pulpit was declared vacant May 18th, 1851.

During the pastorate of Dr. Wilson, there were added to this church forty persons.

Geo Duffield Jr

VI.

REV. GEORGE DUFFIELD, JR., THE FIFTH PASTOR.*

THE church being again without a pastor, began earnestly to look about for one who, it was thought, would not only excite confidence in the present membership, but add largely to its numbers and efficiency. Mr. Isaac Ashmead, one of the elders, suggested that, according to what he had learned, Rev. George Duffield, Jr., was such a person as the church needed.

Accordingly, Messrs. Ashmead, B. D. Stewart and Wm. Sanderson, visited Bloomfield, N. J., where Mr. Duffield was then stationed as a pastor. This committee remained over the Sabbath at that place, and attended the church where Mr. Duffield was officiating. On their return they gave such an account of Mr. Duffield, as led the Session of the church to extend an invitation to him to come and occupy their pulpit for a Sabbath, and administer the communion. This invitation was extended through Rev. Dr. Malin. At the same time, Mr. J. A. Spencer, on behalf of the congregation wrote, inquiring of Mr.

---

* Rev. George Duffield, Jr , was born in Carlisle, Pa. He graduated at Yale College in 1837, when he entered Union Theological Seminary, N. Y., where he graduated in the year 1840. His licensure and ordination took place about the same time He became pastor of a new church in Brooklyn, L. I., where he remained about seven years, when he went to Bloomfield, N. J., where he continued until called to this church Since leaving here he has been pastor of the churches at Adrian, Mich., Galesburg, Ill., and Saginaw City, Mich. The latter charge he has been compelled to resign, owing to sickness.

Duffield if he would entertain a call from this church. In reply, Dr. Malin received the following letter:

Bloomfield, Nov. 4th, 1851.

MY DEAR BROTHER:—Yours of the 31st ult., containing a request of the elders of the Central Presbyterian Church, N. L., to visit them next Sabbath and administer the communion, came duly to hand, and would have been answered before but for a distressing accident that has confined me constantly to the bed-side of my little son * * * In such circumstances you will readily perceive that I cannot be with the church next Sabbath. For this they are probably prepared by a letter, which I wrote to Mr. J. A. Spencer last week.

The fact, my dear brother, is simply this: From the first time this subject was fairly presented to my mind, I have endeavored carefully to watch the indication of God's providence in reference to it. God, I trust, has given me many seals of my ministry here, and certainly the field is a very important one. I have no reason to leave, no desire to leave, unless I can do so for one still larger and more important. I do not want to *put myself* in any place. Wherever the *Great Head of the Church puts me*, I trust I am willing to live, and I hope willing to die also.

Meanwhile, that my relations here may not be unpleasantly affected, I have determined to act with the full understanding and advice of the members of my Session. If I should receive a call, they are willing that I should consider it; willing that I should go to Philadelphia and preach there; willing even that *I should go*, if the path of duty is made plain before me. But, they are not willing I should *invite* a call, or in any way compromise myself beforehand. With kind regards, &c.,

(Signed) GEORGE DUFFIELD, JR.

Extract of a letter to Mr. J. A. Spencer.

Bloomfield, N. J., Oct. 29th., 1851.

As to the subject of your letter, I can only say, that the principle on which I wish to act, is, to judge of nothing before the time. "He that judgeth a matter before he heareth it," you know, "it shall be a shame unto him." I have no will, or wish in the premises, but simply to know my duty. If you should extend a call to me, and after spending a Sabbath with you, the congregation should be inclined unanimously to ratify it, I should feel it necessary to give the subject a very solemn, candid, and prayerful consideration.

Further than this, I have nothing to say at present; and this I am willing all should know, who are in any way interested in the matter.

(Signed) GEO. DUFFIELD, JR.

These communications from Mr. Duffield, were read at a meeting of the congregation, held Nov. 12th, 1851; whereupon, the people recommended the Session to call a congregational meeting, on Monday evening, Nov. 17th, for the election of a pastor. This meeting was duly called, and with entire unanimity, Rev. Geo. Duffield, Jr., was elected pastor, and Messrs. S. T. Bodine, R. M. Foust and J. A Spencer, were appointed commissioners to prosecute the call.

After the call had been presented, Mr. Duffield visited this church, and preached for the people.

Again the congregation was called together, and on Dec. 10th, 1851,

Resolved, That having had an opportunity to see and here Rev. Geo. Duffield, Jr., do hereby ratify and confirm their action of a former meeting, extending a call to him to become their pastor.

Mr. Duffield formally signified his acceptance of the call, Dec. 14th, 1851. Shortly after this, the pastor elect began his labors amongst the people, but was not regularly installed until May 13th, 1852.

The pastor's salary in the call was fixed at $1500 per annum; the pews at that time yielding an annual revenue of $2200.

The church received their new pastor gladly; and the records show that with much cordiality and mutual zeal, pastor and people joined hands in the work of the church.

The people had felt the unexpected removal of Dr. Wilson from among them. Many had become disheartened and left; but yet, there was at the time of Mr. Duffield's installation, a good congregation, and many hopeful indications for the future.

An early effort was put forth to liquidate the entire debt of the church. Appeals were made to the people, and contributions solicited; these, however, terminated quite short of success.

The tide of population which had before this commenced, continued to move westward. This affected very materially the pew rentals, and compelled the trustees to adopt other means to increase the revenue of the church. Needed alterations in the church property were paid for by voluntary subscription. All expenses where it was possible were cut down.

The foreclosure of a mortgage of $6000, held by an outside party, was threatened; but this was prevented by persons inside of the church purchasing it. The constant removal of members to other parts of the city, and their connecting themselves with other churches nearer their new homes, was the occasion of much discouragement.

It became the conviction of many, that the church could no longer exist in the neighborhood. An impression obtained in the community that the congregation was ready to sell the property. A communication was received Jan. 10th, 1853, from the Board of Trustees of the Union Presbyterian Church in the Northern Liberties, stating they had understood the church was for sale, and asking the terms and time of sale. (This Union Presbyterian Church was organized in October, 1852, under the pastoral care of Rev. Mr. Durnett. Those constituting it were a colony from the First Presbyterian Church, N. L. The congregation worshiped for a time in the Old Lecture Room in Coates street, above Second; afterwards in a hall at the S. E. corner of Ninth and Spring Garden streets. Not making the progress hoped for, the church was soon disbanded.)

Although the congregation voted that the property was not for sale, yet the communication shows the opinion which was current in the community.

From this time, as the records show, the subject of removal became a topic for frequent discussion in the meetings of Session, in the meetings of the Board of Trustees, and in the meetings of the congregation. At several of these meetings we find the subject introduced, as a matter for general conversation; at others, it is presented in what were demominated "test resolutions."

At a special meeting of the congregation, held June 18th, 1855, the subject was brought directly before the people by the following resolution:

Resolved. That we deem it expedient to sell this church, with a view of removing to another location.

Pending this question, a statement was made by a committee, appointed at a joint meeting of the Session and the Trustees; accompanying this, was the following written statement from the pastor:

"Since the announcement ot this meeting last Sabbath, it has occurred to me, that as a statement was about to be presented by the Session and Trustees to the congregation, it might be equally appropriate on my part to make a similar statement, should it be called for, as your pastor. By all whom it may concern, either now or hereafter, I would wish it distinctly to be understood:

1st. That my relations to the Trustees and Session of the church, up to the present time, have been uniformly cordial and satisfactory.

2d. That the inception of this movement did not originate with me, but with the Trustees and Session.

3d. That it did not originate *indirectly* with me, by the pressure of any pecuniary claims.

4th. That according to the best judgement I am able to form in the premises, the circumstances of the case are such as to warrant the step that has been taken in laying them before the congregation.

And now that the church itself, alike in its officers and members, may be relieved as far as possible from any embarrassment in the matter, I beg leave to notice,

1st. Some of the more obvious *contingencies* that may arise.

2d. The *relations* I am willing to sustain to each of these as an individual.

The *possible* contingencies are mainly three.

1st. To change the location of the church in such a manner, as to preserve the existing congregation still unbroken, and so draw in *new* strength without diminishing the old.

2d. Amicably to divide, and allow each portion of the church as thus divided, to take such a course as they think proper.

3d. In case these arrangements should fail, to remain where we are.

The relations which I am willing to sustain to these several plans are as follows:

1st. Hereby to tender my resignation at the outset, if by so doing the ultimate establishment of the church can be secured.

2d. To subscribe to the full amount of my ability for the erection of another edifice.

3d. Provided a sufficient sum can first be secured to warrant such an effort, to do all that I can to obtain any further assistance that may be needed from the church at large.

4th. In all other respects I shall be mainly guided.

I trust, by that which will best promote the temporal and spiritual welfare of a church which has already done much for the cause of Christ in this part of the city, and which, I sincerely hope, is destined yet to do a great deal more.

Heavily as the burden has pressed upon many of you, you have been abundantly rewarded for it, both in your own souls and in your families.

If you have sowed temporal things, you have reaped spiritual, and your labor has not been in vain in the Lord.

Believing that you will fully appreciate the motives that have prompted me to this communication, I remain, with sincere and unabated affection,

(Signed) GEO. DUFFIELD, JR., *Pastor.*

After hearing the views of the pastor, the Session, and the Trustees, the congregation appointed from among their own number (other than members of the Session or Board of Trustees) seven persons as a committee to take the subject into consideration, and report at a subsequent meeting.

On the 25th of June, 1855, this committee made their report. After enumerating all the difficulties in the way of remaining in their present location, or removing to another, they close their report with the following:

Resolved, That no corporation, church or business enterprise can succeed whose expenses excel its income.

Resolved, That we deem it expedient to dispose of this church property to some evangelical denomination, with a view to remove to another location.

After considerable discussion on the second resolution, the whole matter was laid over to an adjourned meeting, held July 9th, 1855, when the resolution was further discussed, amended, and passed in the simple form in which, on June 18th, Mr. Henry Davis had presented it, namely:

Resolved, That we deem it expedient to sell this church, in view of removing to another location.

Although the congregation did not commit themselves, by resolution, to any specified locality, it may be interesting to know that the sentiment expressed and recorded at that time was that the location should be between Sixth and Eighth, and Green and Poplar streets. Believing that these streets would mark the boundaries, and anticipating some future action of the congregation, Mr. B. D. Stewart, one of the elders of the church (some time prior to the occurrences of which we now speak), secured the control of a lot on the east side of Seventh street, and north of Brown street, the one now occupied by the Second Reformed Church. This control he held for more than two years, but seeing no active steps taken for removal, and being unsupported by others in the congregation, he allowed it to pass into the hands of those who now hold it.

The passage of the resolution to sell and remove, if it did no more at the time, kept the matter from further agitation in the church; for we look in vain through the records of years to find even a reference to the subject.

This was not because of any increase in the prosperity of the church, for, numerically and financially, it appears from the several reports made to the congregation, it was year after year growing weaker. To keep it in existence, we find various means adopted. Sinking funds were created. The people were called upon, time and again, for extra contributions. The ladies undertook to make good the pastor's salary. With all these efforts, the deficiencies became alarming. We find in the report given at a meeting held November 19th, 1860, that the annual receipts amounted to but $1,200, while the annual indebtedness was $2,400.

The pastor sympathized fully with the people in their embarrassments, and acceded to their desires, by accepting a salary of $1,000 per annum.

All these efforts, however, were too feeble to resist the logic of circumstances. People possessed with means were continually removing to the northern and western sections of the city.

Dismissions and commendations to other churches were constantly being asked for, and given to the members. The impression gained ground that the days of the church were numbered. In the Presbytery, in the church, and in the community, its existence much longer was despaired of. Some there were who proposed to disband; but at a meeting of the congregation, held November 12th, 1860, more from a desire to continue than an assurance that continuance was possible, it was

Resolved, That this congregation disclaim all intention of disbanding as a church.

With a will the remnant of this Israel worked together, and God be praised for the resolute hearts he gave them to hold together, when all their efforts seemed so hopeless.

It is pleasing to turn from a dark to a bright pic ture. This we do when we turn from the temporal to the spiritual affairs of the church. These years of toil and struggle were marked with God's presence in the sanctuary. Mr. Duffield was earnest in the preaching of the gospel. That preaching was not in vain. Turning from the business records of the Board of Trustees and congregation, to the Sessional records of the church, we find how sinners converted were being added regularly to the church.

The "Great Revival" which spread over so many parts of our country during the winter of 1857 and the spring of 1858, was felt very powerfully by this church. The members of the church were greatly quickened in their religious feelings. Meetings were appointed for every night in the week, and for several consecutive weeks these meetings continued with unabated interest. Many of the members of the church superintended and sustained religious services in fire engine houses, and other places where opportunity offered. So general and so controlling was the influence of the Holy Spirit, that *all the people* were aroused to work. The full extent of this work we cannot tell; but this church, as a result, rejoiced in receiving into its membership, on profession of faith, 71 persons.

Mr. Duffield continued to minister to this people until June 19th, 1861. At that time, agreeably to notice given from the pulpit on the preceding Sabbath, a congregational meeting was held, and the following communication from the pastor was read:

To the Central Presbyterian Church, N. L., Phila.

DEAR BRETHREN:—For reasons already fully assigned, entirely satisfactory, I trust, to the brethren, and which it is unnecessary now to repeat, I herewith respectfully tender my resignation as the pastor of the Central Presbyterian Church, N. L. Agreeably to the "Form of Government," Chapter XVII, I would also request the congregation to appear, by their commissioners, at the next meeting of the Fourth Presbytery, to show cause, if any they have, why the Presbytery should not accept said resignation.

Yours, in the fellowship of the gospel,

GEORGE DUFFIELD, JR.

PHILADELPHIA, June 16, 1861.

The congregation acceded to the request of their pastor, and appointed Messrs. Wm. Sanderson and Geo. C. Bower a committee to represent them in Presbytery.

At the same time they appointed a committee to draft resolutions expressive of the views of the people with regard to their pastor. This committee reported the following:

Jas G. Mitchell

Resolved, That in accepting the resignation of our pastor, the Rev. George Duffield, Jr., we take the opportunity to bear witness to his unwearied labors for our spiritual welfare, his Christian deportment, and disinterested self-devotion to the cause of religion and morality in our midst for the past nine years; and we hope that wherever, in the providence of God, he may be called to labor, that the blessing of Heaven may attend his efforts.

This resolution was adopted, and a copy sent to Mr. Duffield.

At a meeting of the Fourth Presbytery, held on the 27th of June, 1861, the dissolution of the pastoral relation between Mr. Duffield and this people was formally consummated.

During the nine years of Mr. Duffield's labors in this church, there were added to its communion 237 persons.

VII.

THE REV. JAMES Y. MITCHELL, THE SIXTH PASTOR.*

The church again without a pastor, depended upon such supplies as could be secured. The inconvenience

---

* Mr. Mitchell was born in this city. From Harrison Grammar School, he was admitted into the High School, where he was a student for about three years. Upon leaving the High School, he entered the Academy at Newark, Del., where he was prepared for college. After spending two years in Delaware College, he entered Union College, Schenectady, N. Y., where he graduated July 26th, 1854. In the fall of the same year, he entered Princeton Theological Seminary, and continued there until graduation, May 12th, 1857. He was licensed to preach the gospel by the Philadelphia Presbytery in April, 1857. While in the Seminary he received and accepted a call from the Presbyterian Church at Phillipsburg, N. J., and on July 14th, 1857, was ordained, and installed pastor of the same by Newton Presbytery. He continued with his first church until January, 1862.

and difficulty attendant upon securing different ministers every week, induced the Session to arrange for the supply of their pulpit for a longer period by the same person. This arrangement after the lapse of a few months, did not give very general satisfaction, and the pulpit was again opened for other ministers to be heard.

It was in the month of February, 1862, that the Session invited Rev. James Y. Mitchell to preach for them. Mr. Mitchell at that time was making his home with his parents in the city. Having resigned the pastoral charge of the Presbyterian Church at Phillipsburg, N. J., on the first Sabbath in January, 1862, he was now desirous of enjoying a season of rest from pastoral duties. Upon coming to the city, he was invited to preach in the First Presbyterian Church, N. L. In this Church he had been baptized in infancy, and in this church he had continued until he left home to pursue his studies for the ministry. The pastor of the First Church, N. L., being ill at the time, Mr. Mitchell concluded to take his place in the pulpit. It was whilst temporarily supplying this pulpit that several members of the Central N. L. Church, some of whom were formerly schoolmates and associates with Mr. Mitchell, heard him, and to them is due the invitation which he soon received to occupy their pulpit.

Beginning in February, 1862, he preached, upon weekly invitations, almost without interruption until the month of May, when he was absent for several weeks as a commissioner from the Presbytery of Newton to the General Assembly, then sitting at Columbus, Ohio. Upon his return, however, the invitations were renewed, and his preaching continued.

During these months he was frequently spoken to about becoming the pastor of this church. At that time, he freely stated his misgivings about settling in the city. He feared that coming to his native place, laboring under the shadow of his father's house, having in his congregation, and among the office bearers of his church, those who knew him in the thoughtlessness of his youth, would impair his efficiency as a minister of the gospel. But there were dreadful misgivings about the church itself. There were less than one hundred reliable names upon the church register; a debt amounting to $7500 still rested against the property; the pew rents barely yielded $1000; and there was little encouragement to gather a congregation from the surrounding German community. While investigating the condition of things, daily was mention made of the hopelessness of the enterprise. In the Pastor's Association, in the Presbytery, in the surrounding churches and community, the church was spoken of as having a *bare existence*, but not a life; and prominent ministers were not slow to say, "it would be folly for the congregation to call another pastor."

Over against these misgivings, however, was the fact, that, though small in numbers, the congregation had determination, courage, and much prayer. The people were earnest, faithful and ready to make sacrifices; and the cordiality with which Mr. Mitchell's companions of other days greeted him, gave assurance that the friendships, the allowances, and the sympathies of early days, might be carried into manhood life; that they who have schooled together, and played together, when lads, could work together, pray together, and be taught together in the house of God.

Encouraged in the matter, the congregation at a a meeting duly called on June 11th, 1862, elected Rev. James Y. Mitchell their pastor, at a salary of $1000 per annum, and Messrs. Wm. Sanderson and Robert M. Foust were appointed a committee to prosecute the call before Presbytery.

Upon the reception of the call, Mr. Mitchell addressed the following letter to the Board of Trustees, which they in turn presented to the congregation, at a meeting held July 16th, 1862.

Philadelphia, July 5th, 1862.

BRETHREN.—Through you I desire to signify to the congregation of the Central Presbyterian Church, N. L., my acceptance of the call to become their pastor. Whatever objections may have suggested themselves to my mind at first, I believe have been fully removed by the following information:

1st. The debt on your church edifice is in such hands as to warrant the belief that it will give you no present trouble, and also that the said debt will speedily be removed altogether.

2d. Your congregation, though small compared with what it once was, is a *united* congregation, and I can rely on this unity in my endeavors to build up your enterprise.

For our mutual understanding, I request at the outset, from you, an assent to the following propositions:

1st. Punctual payment of each quarter's salary.

2d. An increase of salary at such time when the revenue of the church from pew rents will justify it.

3d. A vacation of four weeks during the summer season of each year.

4th. A cordial co-operation with me in the work of building up the Redeemer's kingdom.

It is becoming in me to state that I enter upon the work with fear and trembling, and nothing fortifies me in accepting your call but the assurance that God can bring strength out of weakness.

I have sought for light, by means of consultation, meditation and prayer; and directed, as I trust I have been, by the Blessed Spirit, may my mingling with you hereafter, as your pastor, be blessed to us all.

Desirous of hearing from you with regard to my propositions, I am,

Your brother in Christ,

(Signed) JAS. Y. MITCHELL.

The congregation having assented to the propositions contained in the above letter, Mr. Mitchell began his labors at once.

It was not, however, until October of the same year that he made application for and received his letter of dismission from Newton Presbytery. This letter was presented to the Fourth Presbytery of Philadelphia, October 15th, 1862, and Mr. Mitchell's name was ordered to be enrolled as a member of said Presbytery.

On October 26th, 1862, he was installed as pastor of this church. Notwithstanding a heavy rain kept many away, quite a large audience gathered to witness the installation, and encourage, by their presence, the efforts of the people to continue the worship of God where in other days he had so signally blessed them.

The report which was read at the first annual meeting of the congregation succeeding the installation, speaks very encouragingly of the condition of things in the church at that time. The congregations were considerably larger, while the pew rentals had increased, and the prospects generally were more encouraging.

At this time it was thought that the good of the church might be promoted by fostering a more sociable feeling among the members. To this end, meetings were held every Tuesday evening, at the houses of the members. Beneficial results accrued from these meetings. The people became better acquainted with each other; the interests of the church were kept continually before them, and weekly collections were voluntarily made to supplement the regular revenues of the church.

Notwithstanding the efforts which were being

made, the deficiencies in the receipts were not met; and, by a vote of the congregation, a committee was appointed to canvass it, in order to procure such subscriptions as the members were willing to give, in addition to what they were already contributing. This was the beginning of what was known as the "Quarterly Subscriptions." Due notice was given from the pulpit of the time these subscriptions were to be paid, and the congregation became as familiar with the notice of their payment being due, as they were with the quarterly announcement of "the pew committee being in attendance to receive pew rents now due; also, to rent pews and sittings."

"Quarterly Subscriptions" became a fixed fact during the continuance of the congregation in the "Old Church." It became evident that the debt of $7,500 against the property should, if possible, be at once liquidated. To this end the attention of the people was early called. The pastor was requested to see the mortgage holders, and learn whether they would be willing to make any abatement of their claims. Some were quite ready so to do at once. Others had to be more frequently seen. After a time they all gave encouragement by donating the back interest, and relinquishing, in whole or part, the principal. Finding also a willingness on the part of many outside of the church to contribute towards the liquidation of the entire indebtedness, a meeting of the congregation was informally called, on Wednesday evening, April 8th, 1863. At this meeting, the people, upon learning of the liberality of the creditors, and of others in the community, determined to go to work and see what they could do as individuals. Many took subscription books to go among their friends; many subscribed themselves; and so resolute were they in the matter, that the week following the Board of Trustees, at an adjourned meeting, appointed a committee to receive moneys brought in by the people, and to attend to the paying off the debt. The whole indebtedness was virtually provided for in two weeks, and in one month from the commencement of the effort the claims against the church were satisfied.

The debt which had oppressed the people from the beginning of the enterprise was removed, and the committee of the Board found that they had received $226.45 more than was required.

This work was the work of a people interested, determined, and laboring in unity.

Many were the thanksgivings offered unto God for this timely relief, and many were the expressions of gratitude, not only because of the work done, but because also of the manner in which it was done.

All had done what they could.

The people united in an expression of good-will and friendship towards their pastor, and on the 24th of May, 1863, gave him, as a token of their kindly feelings, a beautiful gold watch, suitably engraved, to perpetuate the memories of those glad days.

The congregation had not yet ceased to believe

that at an early date, necessity would compel them to change the location of the church. God seemed to be arranging for the removal. Now that the debt was removed, the whole subject was simplified.

The trustees turned their attention to getting a full possession of all the pews in the church. It was held that a clear title to the sale of the property could not be given, unless those *owning* pews yielded their claims. A committee of the Board was appointed to arrange this matter. Persons holding "pew deeds" were seen, and soon it was reported that all the deeds were either in the hands of the Board, or the owners were ready cheerfully and fully to return them to the Board.

Now the sale of the church property began to be regularly talked about. The congregation at a meeting held January 9th, 1865, empowered the Board of Trustees to sell the property; they also appointed a committee to obtain a suitable site for a new edifice, together with a committee to receive contributions for a new church. The feeling prevailed that, in locating elsewhere, the wants of the congregation would be best met by going North from Poplar street, and remaining East of Ninth street. Hence, we find reported for consideration, a lot on Franklin street and South of Girard Avenue. This lot was abandoned and another considered at the North-east corner of Eighth street and Girard Avenue.

It was in contemplation at this time, to build a

"Chapel" to answer all present purposes, and wait until some future time for the erection of the main building. The last named lot, containing 90 feet front on Girard avenue, and 140 feet front on Eighth street, seemed to answer the purposes, and met the views of the congregation. The "committee on site," held the refusal of it for a few weeks at $7.00 per foot. During that time the consent of the congregation was given to the purchase of it, and on March 13th, 1865, Messrs. Wm. Sanderson, Wm. R. Stewart, and Abner Lincoln, were appointed "a committee to have erected thereon a suitable building."

When the committee on the purchase of the lot went to the owner to close the bargain, he demanded fifty cents more per foot than he had previously asked; thus breaking his word and disgusting the committee.

This fact occasioned a rest in the agitation of building immediately. All committees appointed with this in view ceased their work, and before the subject was again renewed, by common consent ceased to exist.

The attention of many of the congregation was now turned to the lot at the North-east corner of Franklin and Thompson streets. At that time, there stood on the corner a small, old fashioned and badly dilapitated frame dwelling-house. The balance of the lot was used for the storage of second-hand lumber.

The owner was seen about it several times, but did not feel disposed to sell, because he felt that the requirements of his business demanded him to hold it. The eyes of the congregation were on it, however, and it seemed as though they could not look elsewhere.

In the meantime, the church building was held for sale; but no active steps were taken to hasten it.

The people thought more of what was required in their present position, than of worrying about another. The great need was to hold together those already in the church, and this, under God, was satisfactorily successful.

At a congregational meeting held January 14th, 1867, the Pastor's salary was increased $500 per annum. Although this was the first recorded addition to what was promised him at the beginning, it is to be remembered that regularly, notwithstanding the struggles and sacrifices of the people, they had, up till that time, as they have from that time to the present, annually remembered him with money gifts, varying from $250 to $500.

From the spring of 1865, to that of 1867, little or no mention is made of selling the church property. In the latter year, we find the matter again agitated in the Board of Trustees, and a new committee on sale appointed. The Board at that time fixed the price of the property (with a reservation of part of the church furniture, and the organ) at $20,000. The committee had several interviews with other church committees, who talked of buying, but no definite conclusion was reached. They conferred with a committee of the Fourth Presbytery, who had in charge the purchase of a property for a German Church, but without effecting a sale.

The congregation, on January 13th, 1868, appointed Messrs. S. L. Kirk, Jos. Aitken, Wm. R. Stewart, A. Lincoln and S. Bradbury, "a committee to select a new site, and erect a church edifice thereon."

On May 11th, 1868, Messers. Lincoln and Bradbury, were appointed a committee of the Board of Trustees "to place the church for sale in the hands of a real estate broker, and in the event of his not selling it within a month, to offer it at auction."

Thus it appears, that there was a determination to move; actions tending in this direction were crowding one upon another. The congregation was ever ready to second the action of the Trustees, and the Trustees were ever ready to second the action of the congregation.

Matters took a more definite shape in the summer of 1868. During August, of that year, Mr. Nathan W. Ellis, the owner of the lot at the North-east corner of Franklin and Thompson streets, advised our committee on "purchase of lot" that he was then prepared to sell, and would wait but a limited time before he would offer his lot to the public. Our committee, as soon as the congregation could be brought together after the summer vacation, had a call read for a meeting to be held September 9th, 1868. At this meeting it was stated that the lot on which the people for so long a time had fixed their minds, could now be had; but any failure to act at once, would probably throw it into the hands of others.

With an almost unanimous voice, the people directed its purchase, and appointed Messrs. A. Lincoln and S. Bradbury a committee to secure it on the best terms possible. On the 23d of the same month, the committee reported to the congregation that they had purchased the lot named, 80 feet on Thompson street, and 120 feet front on Franklin street, at $7.50 per foot, making the entire purchase money $15, 000. One half of this amount was to be paid on the execution of the deed, and the other half to remain on mortgage for five years. Immediately upon the determination of the congregation to move, the pastor brought the subject to the attention of the "Pastor's Association. (The "Pastor's Association" was composed of all the pastors in the New School branch of the Presbyterian church, residing in the city of Philadelphia and vicinity). The Association appointed a committee to visit the church, examine its present location and the new site, and report thereon at an early date. The following is their report:

Pastor's Association, Philadelphia,
September 21st, 1868.

The committee appointed to visit the Central Church, N. L., in relation to the proposed removal of the congregation from their present locality on Coates street below Fourth, to another part of the city, beg leave to report, viz.:

The committee on visiting the church, found that the congregation had determined to remove to a lot on Franklin and Thompson streets.

This action we consider profound wisdom.

The present locality of the church, in the midst of an almost entirely German population, and the very many unpleasant surroundings, with little or no material out of which to build up a congregation, lead the committee to the conviction that it must ultimately go down, and that at no very distant day.

This event we all would regard as a great calamity to the cause of Christ, and especially to our branch of the church.

The former history of the Central (N. L.) Church, the benevolence of the members, and their noble work for the Master in years past, deserve to be perpetuated in another and more promising field—one in which their energies can be put forth on more hopeful material than its present locality will ever afford.

The lot on the corner of Franklin and Thompson streets, on which they propose to build a new and handsome house of worship, the committee regard as a very excellent position. It is in a growing portion of the city, surrounded by a population of the highest respectability, more than a mile distant from the nearest church of our denomination, and more convenient for the congregation now attending the old church.

With the spirit which the prospect of a new and more hopeful field has infused into the congregation, the energy of their pastor, Rev. James Y. Mitchell, and the blessing of God, the committee feel that a flourishing and influential congregation will be the result of the removal to this point.

In view of this fact, and the good work which this old church has already done for Presbyterianism, and unwilling to see its light go out for want of a proper field in which to expand its power for good, we cordially commend this enterprise to the warm sympathy and Christian liberality of our people, trusting to make the latter history of the Central Church more glorious than the former.

(Signed) R. H. Allen,
Herrick Johnson,
Peter Stryker,
Geo. F. Wiswell,
Z M. Humphrey,
} *Committee.*

This report encouraged the people, as they felt that they had the sympathy and co-operation of the Christian community, and that with these, success must surely come.

They appointed Messrs. A. Lincoln, J. F. Jaggers, and the pastor, a committee to solicit subscriptions in the congregation; and Mr. S. L. Kirk, Treasurer, to receive all moneys collected, by the committee or congregation, for the new church.

An unlooked-for event happened about this time. The Session, at the request of the pastor, called a meeting of the congregation, October 14th, 1868, for the purpose of getting the people to unite with him in asking Presbytery to dissolve the relation existing between him and this church.

The meeting was held in accordance with the call,

and, by a unanimous vote, the congregation decided to remonstrate against such a dissolution, and appointed Messrs. Jos. Aitken, Abner Lincoln, and Robert Aitken, commissioners to represent them in Presbytery. The elders were appointed a committee to wait upon the pastor, acquaint him with the action of the congregation, and report at a subsequent meeting, to be held on Friday evening, October 16th, 1868. At this meeting the elders reported having seen Mr. Mitchell, and that the whole matter had been satisfactorily adjusted.

Mr. Mitchell, upon invitation of the congregation, made a short address, in which he expressed the happy relations which had existed between him and his people since he had become their pastor; expressed the hope that the subject which had agitated them would speedily be forgotten, and that together they might labor in happy accord for the welfare of the church. The occasion of his application to be relieved was not sought for, nor was it in the line of his own judgment. Several of his ministerial brethren had named a place in Michigan as the key to the whole of the Northwest, and as a place of great importance to Presbyterianism. Believing that he had the necessary qualifications to improve it to the best advantage of the church and kingdom of Christ, they desired him to go there. Taking the advice of these brethren, and having flattering inducements held out to him by a people he had never seen, he yielded his own judgment, and sought to acquiesce in theirs.

This congregation, however, interfered, and showed their appreciation of their pastor not only by a congregational vote, but also by adding to his salary $1000.

It should ever be remembered, that while they were struggling towards the building of a new church, they made this increase of salary, and the Lord enabled them to meet it as readily as any they had ever paid before.

On November 2d, 1868, the congregation authorized the Board of Trustees to execute a mortgage to Nathan W. Ellis for $7,500, for five years from January 1st, 1869; and at a subsequent meeting, held November 27th, 1868, authorized the Board of Trustees to build a new church edifice on the lot purchased, to make contracts, and to incur all necessary expenses in so doing.

VIII.

THE "OLD EDIFICE" SOLD, AND THE "NEW ONE" BUILDING.

The records of the Board show that they were now earnestly engaged in furthering the wishes of the congregation.

At their regular stated meeting, held February 8th, 1869, Messrs. S. L. Kirk, Abner Lincoln, and S. Bradbury, were, on motion of Mr. Wm. R. Stewart.

appointed "The Building Committee." This committee invited the pastor to co-operate with them.

The Building Committee held several interviews with Mr. Addison Hutton, architect, giving him certain general outlines as to the kind of building they desired; specifying certain particulars which they had seen in other churches they had visited, and which they desired to have in our own; and finally reported to the Board, April 12th, 1869, that they had adopted the plans and specifications furnished by Mr. Hutton; had received estimates based upon these plans and specifications, and that other builders were estimating upon them.

The committee, in arranging with the architect, desired not only that he should prepare plans and specifications, but that he should put these into the hands of but a limited number of builders, and these of unquestionable standing; that he should give his attention to the building as it progressed, and see that it was built of the best materials and in the most workmanlike manner; and that in all cases of dispute which might arise between the contractor and committee, he should act as arbiter. The committee engaged to pay him for his services, in these several particulars, a percentage on the cost of the building, which, when a final settlement was made, amounted to $1,950.

From the time when the new lot was purchased, the disposal of the church property became a subject of great perplexity. It was felt that no work on the new building could go on until money had been secured from the sale of the old. The Committee on sale were necessarily laboring with many misgivings. There had been much advertising of the old property for sale, but no buyers were found. Real estate brokers could not, or did not dispose of it. As a last resource, it was placed in the hands of Thomas & Sons, auctioneers, to be sold November 24th, 1868, at public sale, with the understanding that it should not be sold for less than $15,000.

None can imagine the surprise and mortification experienced by the committee in attendance upon that sale, when, after many efforts on the part of the auctioneer, not a single bid could be secured, even at the low figure named.

The work of that day made hearts sick. It was felt that the property must be disposed of now, at any price. Spring, and with it the time of building would soon come. It had been noised abroad that the work on the new building would soon commence; but how could it now, when the *unsold property* held us back. Our hopes for the time seemed blasted.

Just when matters were at the worst, God interfered. A committee from the Salem Reformed (German) Church, held a conference with the committee of this church, with regard to the purchase of the property. At this conference, they asked for and obtained the refusal of the property for one week. At that time, April 27th, 1869, the committees again met, and after a season of conference, the property on Coates street was sold to the Salem German Reformed Church, for $17,750.

In this sale was included all the property, with the exception of pulpit furniture, communion table, and such other goods as might be denominated Sabbath School, or private property. The terms of sale were such as to allow the building committee to go forward in their work with satisfaction, as soon as the season would permit.

The relief which this sale afforded was opportune, and, as we believe, directed by the unerring wisdom of God. Had any questioned the propriety of changing location, God in this matter convinced them by a voice which said "go forward."

The Sabbath following this relief, the pastor understanding the feelings of the people, and entering into the channel of their thoughts, preached from the text, "The cloud was taken up from over the tabernacle," Exodus, 40 chap. 36 verse. The directions and deliverences of God, were presented in the sermon; and the people were taught to see that by command of God, they were to go up and possess the new land. Before that Sabbath day had closed, one young man who before that time had not seen his way clear to give to the new enterprise, sent a letter to the pastor, stating that he was fully convinced the Lord had determined the movement, and enclosed a substantial donation to help it forward.

A lady also, who prior to that time had opposed any change in location, after hearing of the providences of God, which had confirmed the wisdom of the change, resolved, that should the Lord ever put in her possession a certain sum of money which had been owing to her for a long time, she would give *it* as a contribution towards the new church. Strange to say, within a few days from the time she made the resolution, she had received the money and given it over for the object named.

The "Old Building" having now been sold, the work of going forward with the "New" was stimulated. The estimates for finishing the entire building when opened and read, were found to be considerably beyond the calculations of the Building Committee, ranging as they did from $67,000 to over $80,000. It was then concluded to invite estimates for the putting up of the building, roofing it in, topping out the tower, flooring the audience room, and finishing the Lecture Room complete.

In estimating upon this work, Mr. Robert Scott, of Wilmington, Delaware, was the lowest bidder; and with him, Abner Lincoln, President, and Robert Aitken, Secretary, on behalf of the Board of Trustees, contracted for the building of an edifice according to the plans and specifications of Addison Hutton, Architect.

It was on Tuesday, May 11th, 1869, when Mr. Scott's estimate was accepted by the Building Committee. At the Wednesday evening lecture, the congregation was invited to meet before 7 o'clock on Thursday morning, May 13th, on the lot at Franklin and Thompson streets. A goodly number met at the time named, when the pastor, in prayer, invoked the Divine blessing upon the enterprise; prayed that there might be no interruption for want of means to go forward; asked protection for all who might labor on or about the building, so that no accident might befall any; and entreated the Heavenly Father to make the church there erected, a lasting good to the community, and a glory to his holy name.

After prayer, the pastor took a spade, dug the first earth, and cast it into a cart. He was followed by the other members, male and female, and soon the first cart load of earth was hauled away.

From that time the work went steadily forward. All were solicitous about the kind of soil which would be found beneath the surface. We were gladdened to see it all that we could desire; and the universal testimony was, that no better *foundation* for a building could be found anywhere.

The walls rest upon a coarse, gravelly bed, which packs into a solidity by a pressure bearing upon it. The first stone was laid by the pastor on the morning of June 9th, 1869, at the northwest corner of the foundation walls. The season was remarkably favorable for building, and, with but slight interruptions, a large gang of masons continued their work, having the walls ready for the reception of the first floor joists in the beginning of July.

It had been arranged to have appropriate services at the laying of the Corner Stone. Invitations were extended to many of the friends of the enterprise to be present; and, through the papers, the public was invited to meet on the afternoon of July 8th, 1869, to witness the ceremony.

A temporary floor had been laid upon the first floor joists, and near the southwest corner of the building a canopy had been raised, under which seats were arranged for clergymen and ladies.

The afternoon was excessively warm; not a cloud softened the burning rays of that July sun. People chose rather to be within doors, yet, notwithstanding the heat, a large crowd gathered to witness the ceremonies. Many clergymen, representing different denominations, took seats in the places assigned them. The ladies, in large numbers, graced the scene with their presence; and either standing in the crowd, or resting on extemporized seats, or grouping at the windows of houses opposite, were people in numbers sufficient to give enthusiasm to the occasion.

The exercises consisted of singing, under the direction of Mr. Joseph F. Jaggers; prayer; reading of the Scriptures; and short addresses by visiting clergymen. The pastor then read a condensed history of the church; after which he placed in a beautiful glass casket (made expressly for this occasion, and presented by the manufacturers, Gillenger & Bennett), a copy of the Bible; Confession of Faith; *The American Presbyterian; The Presbyterian;* copies of all our city daily papers; a set of proof coins (a gift from Mr. John Campbell, of Manayunk); the history which he had just read, and the names of the church members. The casket was then deposited in the Corner-Stone, and covered with a large stone slab. Then the pastor struck the stone three times with a mason's mallet, and publicly announced the Corner-Stone laid, in the name of the Father, Son and Holy Ghost. After the audience had sung a hymn, they were dismissed with the Apostolic Benediction.

The Corner-Stone was laid in the southwest corner of the building (on a line with the first floor joists), in the tower, immediately behind the angle formed by the two buttresses on that corner; the one facing south on Thompson street, and the other facing west on Franklin street.

The history read on this occasion, and deposited in the Corner-Stone, is introduced at this point. For although it repeats some few facts already recorded, it presents new matter, and will furnish links to what might otherwise be detached history.

HISTORY.

"The corporate title of this church is 'The Central Presbyterian Church in the Northern Liberties.'

"The original limits of Philadelphia were the Delaware and Schuylkill rivers, east and west, and Vine and Cedar streets, north and south.

"All above Vine street was called 'North End,' and below Cedar street, 'South End,' or 'Society Hill.' With the growth of society in these sections, separate municipalities became necessary, and the 'South End' became the municipality of 'Southwark,' and the 'North End' the municipality of the 'Northern Liberties.' The district of the Northern Liberties was incorporated in the year 1803, and was not consolidated with the city until the year 1854. At the time of its incorporation its population numbered about 16,000, and at the time of its consolidation about 60,000 inhabitants.

"During the latter half of the last century the spiritual wants of the people living above the city limits awakened the concern of the Second Presbyterian Church, then worshiping at the corner of Third and Arch streets. This church was part of the fruits of the great revival under Whitefield's preaching, and was characterized for its zeal to propagate the gospel. It still survives the change of years, and it is worthy of remark that but about two weeks since, the congregation of the Second Church laid the Corner-Stone for a new church edifice at Twenty-first and Walnut streets. Dr. Beadle is the present pastor.

"Rev. Dr. Sproat, who succeeded Rev. Gilbert Tennent, D.D., the first pastor of the Second Church, instituted religious services in a small house at the northeast corner of St. John and Coates streets. The Revolutionary war interrupted these services; but soon after its close, Dr. Ashbel Green, afterwards President of Princeton College, becoming a colleague of Dr. Sproat, united with him in methodically carrying on the services which had been interrupted. At length the growth of the congregation demanded the building of a church edifice. Mr. Wm. Coates, a large land owner, made donation of the lot on the northwest corner of Second and Coates streets, then open ground, and, as was thought, too remote from the city to be ever disturbed by the march of business. The moneys needed to erect the building were secured by honest begging, and the building finished and opened April 7th, 1805.

"Religious worship was held statedly for eight years, when the growth of the community and wants of the congregation demanded the settlement of a pastor.

"A church was now duly organized, known as the First Presbyterian Church, Northern Liberties, and Rev. James Patterson elected its pastor. He was elected September 27th, 1813, and duly installed on Tuesday, January 11th, 1814.

"The labors of Mr. Patterson were abundantly blessed. He inaugurated new measures to win souls to Christ; he preached Christ in the pulpit and out of the pulpit, in the church and on the commons; he visited much, and sent all his members to visit the sick and distressed. He organized the first Sabbath School; he educated young men for the ministry, and labored in every way for the salvation of men. He saw the number of his communicants rise from 52 to 1,100; and in the twenty-three years of his pastorate in this church 60 young men were introduced into the ministry; 1,700 persons were received into the church; thousands of children instructed gratuitously in Sunday Schools; tens of thousands of immortal ones warned, counseled, exhorted, entreated, in the fields, in the streets, and in the place of prayer.

"In the spring of 1829, it was concluded to sell the old church building at Second and Coates streets, and move into a westward location. This was because of the encroachments of business, and the increasing demands of another locality.

"After the usual trials attending such a movement, the First Presbyterian Church in the Northern Liberties disappeared from the corner of Second and Coates street, but appeared again in Buttonwood street, below Sixth, where the new church building was opened May 12th, 1833.

"Its history has been grand ever since, and to-day it is doing a noble work for God under the pastoral care of Rev. T. J. Shepherd, D.D.

"At the time the moving the old church was first agitated, it had more than a thousand members, and it is not to be wondered at that Christian men should differ as to the best location of a new edifice. Men did differ, and that difference was the origin of the North Presbyterian Church, now standing in Sixth street, above Green, and of the Central Presbyterian Church, N. L., now in Coates street, below Fourth, but which to-day lays the Corner-Stone of a new edifice on this spot.

"Differing from their brethren on the question of church site, and believing they had an independent work to do for their Master, they withdrew from the parent church, and denominating themselves 'The Central Presbyterian Church in the Northern Liberties,' they worshiped for a time in a school-room on Poplar street, above Second, looking, however, to the speedy erection of a church edifice on Coates street, below Fourth. This building, commenced in 1835, was not occupied until the year 1836.

"During the time of its building, the congregation, having left the school-room in Poplar street, worshiped in the old Commissioners' Hall, in Third street, below Green. Here it was that on the 24th day of June, 1835, agreeably to the Form of Government of the Presbyterian Church, 21 persons were organized into a church. Of these 21, six still live, viz.: Hannah R. Naglee, Margaret Stewart, Joseph Aitken, Charles C. Aitken, Joseph Pond, and Catharine Pond—the three first named being still in the communion of the church. At the time of the organization of the church, Rev. John McDowell, D.D., and Rev. Cornelius C. Cuyler, D.D., by invitation, attended. Dr. McDowell presided, and opened the meeting with prayer. After the usual form of questions was proposed to the persons thus presenting themselves, they proceeded to elect, by ballot, three individuals to be ruling elders, when Mr. Charles Elliot, Mr. Benjamin Naglee, and Mr. John A. Stewart, were unanimously elected. The elders elect were then set apart to the office of ruling elders in this church.

"The constitutional questions were proposed to the elders, and to the members, by Dr. McDowell, and were answered in the affirmative, which was followed with prayer by Dr. Cuyler. It was then declared that the church under the name of the Central Presbyterian Church, N. L., was duly organized. This was followed with an address to the elders by Dr. McDowell, and to the church by Dr. Cuyler. The solemn services of the evening were then concluded with the benediction.

"On the 29th of June, 1835, this infant church elected their first pastor, Rev. Wm. H. Burroughs, of New Providence, N. J. Mr. Burroughs soon after accepted the call, and was installed over the church and congregation, by the Second Presbytery of Philadelphia, on the evening of August 24th, 1835. The services were held in the First Presbyterian Church, N. L., by invitation from the pastor, Rev. James Patterson.

"The Sacrament of the Lord's Supper was, for the first time, administered in this infant church July 12th, 1836.

"The labors of Mr. Burroughs in his pastoral charge were of short duration. Disease invaded his system and laid him aside, and soon brought him to his grave. There was a strong mutual attachment between Mr. B. and the people of his charge. He died at Newark, N. J., July 29th, 1836, in the 36th year of his age, greatly beloved and deeply lamented.

"On the 23d of August, 1836, a congregational meeting was held for the purpose of electing a successor to fill the place of Mr. Burroughs. Rev. Thomas A. J. Mines was unanimously elected. Mr. Mines accepted the call, and was installed the September following. He sustained the pastoral relation for a very short period. At the expiration of two months he expressed a desire, in consequence of a feeble state of health, that his pastoral relation be dissolved. The Presbytery agreed to his dismission Mr. Mines continued in a weak and declining state till the 20th of January, 1838, when he was released from his earthly labors.

"For several weeks subsequent to Mr. Mines' dismission, this church did not enjoy the labors of a pastor; they depended on supplies as they were able to secure them.

"On the 23d of October, 1837, the Rev. Anson Rood, of Danbury, Conn., was unanimously elected pastor. Mr. Rood, having accepted the call, was installed December 15th, 1837. The Rev. Eliakim Phelps presided, and proposed the constitutional questions. Rev. John L. Grant preached the sermon. Rev. George Chandler gave the charge to the pastor, and Rev. Albert Barnes the charge to the people. Mr. Rood continued the pastor of the church for eleven years and three months, resigning March 5th, 1849, on account of his health, which, by reason of his labors, had been greatly impaired. His ministry was greatly blessed. Large congregations attended his services. He multiplied these services for the good of souls. He had added to his eldership Mr. Isaac Ashmead, elected October 13th, 1840; also, Messrs. Samuel T. Bodine and William T. Donaldson, who were elected May 8th, 1843, and ordained June 19th of the same year. Frequent were the revivals in the church, and its membership was more than fourfold increased during his ministry. His health continued to fail after his retirement from the active work of the ministry, and he died in the Lord, November 27th, 1857.

"A period of thirteen months elapsed, after the resignation of Mr. Rood, before another pastor was called and installed. On January 4th, 1850, Rev. James P. Wilson, D.D., then President of Delaware College, was elected pastor, and in April of the same year he was installed pastor in the presence of a very large congregation.

"Rev. Joel Parker, D.D., presided, and proposed the constitutional questions; Rev. Dr. Gilbert preached the sermon; Rev. Albert Barnes delivered the charge to the pastor, and Rev. Robert Adair the charge to the people.

"The pastoral relation of Dr. Wilson with his people continued but about fifteen months, when he resigned to accept the Professorship of Systematic Theology in Union Theological Seminary, New York. After serving in that position for some time, he resigned to become pastor of a church in Newark, N. J., where he still resides, in the midst of an admiring and devoted people. His resignation as pastor of this church took place April 8th, 1851.

"About seven months elapsed, when, on November 17th, 1851, Rev. George Duffield, Jr., was elected pastor, and on May 13th, 1852, was duly installed. Dr. Gilbert presided, and proposed the constitutional questions; Dr. James P. Wilson, former pastor, preached the sermon; Rev. George Duffield, Sr., D.D., of Detroit, delivered the charge to the pastor; and Rev. W. W. Taylor the charge to the people.

"Mr. Duffield continued pastor of the church for more than nine years. During this time he was the witness of many revivals, and was fully assured that his faithful preaching of the gospel was accompanied with the power of the Holy Ghost. His soul continually yearned for the salvation of men. He had added to his eldership Messrs. B. D. Stewart, Wm. Sanderson, H. H. Shillingford, and G. C. Bower, who were elected and ordained to office in April, 1855. His resignation took place in the summer of 1861, when he accepted a call to the Presbyterian Church of Adrian, Mich , from which he afterwards went to become the pastor of the Presbyterian Church of Galesburg, Ill., where he still labors, being blessed and blessing others.

"Several months elapsed before another pastor was called. On the 11th day of June, 1862, the congregation elected Rev. James Young Mitchell, then of

Newton Presbytery, N. J. On October 26th following, he was installed as pastor of the church. Rev. T. J. Shepherd, D.D., presided, and proposed the constitutional questions, and delivered the charge to the pastor. Rev. Dr. Brainerd preached the sermon, and Rev. E. E. Adams, D.D., delivered the charge to the people. Up to the present time, for more than seven years, he continues the pastor. He moves with his people in this movement, hoping, trusting, praying, that God will give it success. He has added to his eldership Messrs. Joseph Aitken, James Neely, and Abner Lincoln, who were elected and ordained to office in October, 1866. He has had many occasions to thank God for the outpouring of his Holy Spirit upon his congregation, and for adding to the church a goodly number of such as shall be saved. With thankful heart we record the fact that in the spring of 1863 the last of the debt upon the old church building ($7,500) was removed.

"The old Central Church has done much for the cause of Christ; and though, because of removals to other sections of the city, it has lost many of its once active members, these have not been lost to Christ. Many, if not most of our churches in the city are now enjoying the benefits of faithful workmen, who first began to work for Christ in this old church. Though much of her former glory has departed for the present, we rejoice to believe that the day is not far distant when it will return again. Her existence has not been in vain. Her history is a history of revivals, of large benevolence, and of continued labors for Christ.

"The present movement of our church has long been contemplated. For many years we have suffered much because of our people moving farther north and west. Our church was growing weaker every year. This was said fifteen years ago. The community which we now occupy is largely German. It is becoming more and more so every year. The material to support our church, or to attend it, is not in the neighborhood. We are solicitous for this Zion. It has a grand history. In other days she laid her treasures at the Saviour's feet. She has largely helped to build new churches, and to support feeble ones. No object of Christian obligation, love or charity did she overlook. Multitudes have been saved through her instrumentality—multitudes who have gone up out of her to heaven now swell that great cloud of witnesses which to-day encompasses us; and multitudes more who still linger in this world, pillars in the church of God elsewhere, proudly call it their spiritual birth-place. We have gladdened their hearts, we have gladdened our own, in the transfer of the old edifice in Coates street to German Reformed Salem Church. That old building, where tears of repentance and tears of spiritual joy have been shed, where sinners have been born again and saints been gladdened, where the waters of baptism have been sprinkled and the communion table spread—is not lost to the cause of God. It is still to echo the praises of our Saviour.

"We come to this spot. We come to be more central to our own people. We come to offer further church accommodations to this rapidly growing neighborhood. We come to preach Christ and Him crucified. We lay the Corner-Stone of this new church edifice to day. Soon the last stone will be placed, the last arch sprung, the last beam adjusted.

"When this is done, may we say it is well done! May God say it is well done. May the history and hallowed associations of our time honored church be perpetuated, and when in eternity it is remembered, of many may it be said—They were born there."

"God grant it.—Amen."

The months which followed the laying of the Corner-Stone, were months of considerable anxiety. To the credit of the German committee, we record with pleasure the promptness with which they made every payment upon the old church property as it matured. But, the whole amount which they owed fell far short of the $52,200, the amount due Mr. Robert Scott, upon the contract for building our new church. Our congregation although doing well, could not be expected with their small numbers and limited means, to give as the necessities of the case required.

The building committee held many anxious meetings. It was often felt that the work must cease for want of funds. Not only were there anxious days, but sleepless nights. There was begging and borrowing. It mattered very little, whether there was pouring rain or burning sun, the burden of running the streets soliciting subscriptions and contributions, had to be borne. Ofttimes after the greatest labor of this kind, there was very little to comfort.

At the time the committee of the "Pastors' Association," made their report as previously given, we had hoped to realize from the community, an amount, which added to our own contributions, and the proceeds of the sale of our old property, would be amply sufficient to establish our congregation in the Lecture Room of our new church free from debt. In this we were disappointed.

Growing out of the action of the "Pastors' Association," there was a meeting of prominent Presbyterian laymen called to meet in the Lecture Room of the First Presbyterian Church, Philadelphia, on Washington Square. At that meeting, the financial condition of several of our churches was considered, and a committee consisting of Hon. W. Strong, W. E. Tenbrook, Thomas Potter, Alexander Whilden and John C. Farr, was appointed to examine the matter still further, and report at a subsequent meeting. This committee afterwards reported, recommending the raising of $105,000 to assist or relieve certain churches, which had recently been finished, or were in process of erection. Of this amount our own church was recommended for $25,000. The other churches at the time the committee reported, were more pressed for money immediately, than our own. Hence, of the first contributions made to the fund named, the committee handed over pro rata, to the most needy at the time.

The whole amount of that fund was never raised. Many of the subscriptions were canceled, because the subscribers had given their names on condition that the whole amount be raised, and others of the subscribers donated their individual subscriptions according to their preferences.

One cause which cooled the ardor of the committee and the Presbyterian public, in the matter of raising the whole amount, was the agitation of the "Reunion of the two branches of the Presbyterian Church."

This subject had been for so long a time discussed in church Journals, in Presbyteries, Synods and General Assemblies, that it was a foregone conclusion it must take place. It was actually accomplished at Pittsburgh in 1869.

In the efforts of the committee to make up the fund of $105,000, they found many who hesitated because they believed that upon the "Reunion" an effort would be made to liquidate the debts of all the churches. The committee, because of this public sentiment, measurably failed in their effort to relieve the "New School" churches.

It was not anticipated at that time that a "Reunited Church" would be called upon to do such great things in the way of building a large Presbyterian house, a hospital, a home for widows and single women, and that the demands would be heavy upon the people, for other interests than those of individual churches.

The work of the committee, however, was not lost altogether. The churches which they undertook to relieve, while they did not get what they expected and relied upon, received in part; our own church getting $12,850.

This amount was not actually collected and handed over to our treasurer by the committee. It required personal effort to secure it. The names of the subscribers on the books of the committee were given to the pastor, and either he, or some member of the Building Committee, had to call upon the parties to obtain the amount of their subscriptions. Oftentimes the effort was as trying as the getting of a new contribution.

We cannot but remember, in this connection, our indebtedness to Messrs. Wm. E. Tenbrook, B. D. Stewart, Thomas Potter, Alexander Whildin, and F. L. Bodine (all of whom were either members of the committee or contributors to the fund), for the interest they manifested in our work. To them chiefly we are indebted for the amount which we have received from this source.

Notwithstanding the trials attendant upon raising the means needed to prosecute our work, we experienced no considerable delay. Loans sufficient to bridge over seasons of necessity were from time to time secured. Mr. Abner Lincoln, as the records show, assisted very much in this direction, and to him the church has been, and is still, greatly indebted.

The builders made good use of a remarkably fine summer and fall for building.

Scarcely a working day was interrupted by rain; and so favorable was the season that the roof of the building was completed on December 28th, 1869, and the tower topped out January 4th, 1870.

The work on the inside went on briskly, with the exception of about two weeks in the latter part of February. An agent of the contractor questioned with the Building Committee concerning a payment which he regarded as already due him. The committee differed with him; and pending the dispute, work was suspended. The matter was amicably adjusted in a short time, and the work went on.

According to the terms arranged in the sale of the "old property," our congregation was required, upon the equalization of the payments then agreed upon, to give possession to the German church on October 1st, 1869. Did they not require possession at that time, it was arranged that our congregation should retain possession until March 1st, 1870, upon paying the interest upon the purchase-money from October 1st, 1869 until March 1st, 1870. It was afterwards found that our Lecture Room in the new building would not be ready until later than March; and by an arrangement with the German church, we kept possession of the "Old Building" until April 11th, 1870, we paying interest upon the money received up to that time.

As it grew near the time of leaving the "Old Church," it was thought advisable to have a reunion of the present and former members. To this end the following circular was issued:

"INVITATION.

"*Central Presbyterian Church, (N. L.)*

Coates Street, below Fourth.

"You are affectionately invited to attend a REUNION of the present and former members of the Central Presbyterian (N. L.) Church and congregation, to be held in the church, Coates street, below Fourth, on Thursday evening, March 10th, at a quarter before 8 o'clock.

"This meeting, earnestly desired by many of the former members, and looked forward to with interest by those still in the church, will afford the only opportunity we shall ever have of thus visiting the 'Old Church Building,' so dear to us all because of sweet communions, holy joys and happy associations enjoyed within its walls.

"As a church, we will hereafter remember the days of the past in our new church edifice (now approaching completion) at the northeast corner of Franklin and Thompson streets.

"Let us come together, then, and, in parting at the spot where we have often before so gladly met, may we congratulate each other, and render thanksgiving to God because the 'Old Building,' in passing from us, passes into the hands of the 'Salem German Reformed (German) Congregation,' which will continue to hold it as a place 'where God's honor dwelleth.'

JAMES Y. MITCHELL, *Pastor.*
WM. SANDERSON, SR., }
JOSEPH AITKEN, } *Elders.*
ABNER LINCOLN, }
Committee.

POST OFFICE ADDRESS OF PASTOR, No. 1003 North Fifth street "

This meeting was held, and quite a large number attended. The pastor presided. We had a season of prayer, singing, and reading of the Scriptures. After this, letters were read from Rev. Dr. James P. Wilson, a former pastor, and several of the former members, who were unable to attend.

Pleasant reminiscences of other days were then recounted by Messrs. B. D. Stewart, Henry Davis, G. W. Grice, Duffield Ashmead, Rev. S. W. Duffield, and others; after which all joined heartily in singing the hymn,

"Blest be the tie that binds," &c

when the meeting was closed with the benediction by the pastor.

The German Church took possession of the old property on April 11th, 1870. This was three weeks before our Lecture Room was ready for occupancy. During these three weeks our people visited other churches—watching daily, however, for the announcement in the daily papers of the time when the "opening exercises" would take place in the new edifice.

Everything being in complete readiness, due notice was given in all the city papers on Saturday, May 7th, 1870, that the opening exercises in the Lecture Room would take place on Sabbath, May 8th. Similar notice was given through the *American Presbyterian*, our denominational paper.

The building committee had also prepared a neat folding card, to be sent to individuals who had befriended us, as well as for general distribution in the neighborhood of the church.

On the first page of this card was given the following "Order of Exercises:"

Sunday, May 8th.

SERMONS BY

REV. PETER STRYKER, D.D., Pastor of North Broad Street Presbyterian Church, . . . 10½ A. M.

REV. Z. M. HUMPHREY, D.D., Pastor of Calvary Presbyterian Church, ... 3½ P. M.

REV. H. C. McCOOK, D.D., Pastor of Seventh Presbyterian Church, ... 8 P. M.

Opening of Sabbath School at 2 P. M.

Monday, May 9th.

UNION MEETING.

To be addressed by several neighboring pastors.

SERMONS.

Tuesday, May 10th, at 8 P. M.

REV. HERRICK JOHNSON, D.D., Pastor of First Presbyterian Church.

Wednesday, May 11th, at 8 P. M.

REV. R. H. ALLEN, D.D., Pastor of "Old Pine Street" Presbyterian Church.

Thursday, May 12th, at 8 P. M.

REV. E. R. BEADLE, D.D., Pastor of Second Presbyterian Church.

Friday, May 13th, at 8 P. M.

REV. T. X. ORR, Pastor of First Reformed Church.

Sunday, May 15th, at 10½ A. M.

SERMON BY

REV. R. H. ALLEN, D.D.,

And Administration of the Sacrament of the Lord's Supper.

At 8 P. M.

Sermon by the Pastor.

On the second page of the card was printed the following:

"The Lecture Room of the Central Presbyterian Church, N. L., just completed, at the northeast corner of Franklin and Thompson streets, will be opened with appropriate exercises, commencing Sabbath, May 8th, 1870. You are cordially invited to be present.

JAS. Y. MITCHELL, *Pastor.*"

There was the simplicity of Presbyterian worship maintained at all these services. The Trustees had procured the services of Mr. Joseph F. Jaggers, to lead the singing, and he conducted it after the manner of the Precentor in the Church of Scotland. It was in this way that the singing was conducted at the time the church was opened in Coates street. Then it was under the leadership of Mr. Josiah P. White, who continues his membership with the church until the present time.

The morning of May 8th was beautiful. It appeared as though God had favored us with just such a day as that for which all had been wishing. It was what might have been denominated "a lovely Sabbath morning in spring." The Lecture Room was crowded with worshipers, and all were pleased with the exercises.

About the close of the morning services, clouds began to gather in the sky; the winds rose, and there were many fears that a heavy rain would interfere with the balance of the day's programme. In a measure, our fears became a reality. Rain began to fall a little while after noon; and when the time arrived for the gathering of the Sabbath School scholars, there was not only rain, but there burst upon the city the most terrible and destructive hail-storm ever known in our country. The stones were of an immense size, and were driven by a high wind with such velocity, that protection was sought for by man and beast. So suddenly did it begin, and with such force did it continue, that persons in their homes had not time, nor dared they venture, to close even the shutters, to protect the glass in their windows. This storm, in its fury, continued for at least half an hour; and when it ended, there was scarcely a house which had not its broken window-panes. Some church windows were literally riddled. The number of window-lights broken was calculated, in some of the papers published the next day, at hundreds of thousands, and by others at millions. The Lord saved our church, as two or three small pieces of glass in the borders of the windows were all that were broken.

The storm, which began suddenly, passed away suddenly. When its strength was wasted, the sun shone forth; and although the opening of the Sabbath School was interfered with for a time, we got together at last, and spent a short season with the children in pleasant and profitable opening exercises, directed by Mr. Robert Aitken, superintendent. The remaining parts of the programme were gone through with according to the announcement, with but one exception. It was impossible for Dr. Allen to preach the sermon on Sabbath, May 15th, and the pastor took his place.

At the Union Meeting, on Monday, the 9th, addresses were made by Rev. D. E. Klopp, pastor of Trinity Reformed Church; Rev. Wm. O. Johnstone, pastor of Kensington Presbyterian Church; Rev. J. F. Kennard, pastor of the Tenth Baptist Church; and by the pastor. All the meetings were quite well attended, notwithstanding rains prevailed every evening during the week, with the exception of Friday evening. Collections were taken up at every service, and in the aggregate amounted to $2,880.29, which sum was used to meet, in part, the expenses incurred in the building.

IX.

FROM THE "LECTURE ROOM" TO THE "MAIN AUDIENCE ROOM."

The work done up to the time of the completion of the Lecture Room was in perfect accordance with the original design of the architect, as accepted and approved by the Building Committee, with but slight alterations and additions.

To avoid the annoyance attendant upon outside

drainage from the roof during seasons of rain or snow, the committee, at an additional expense of $275, had iron conductors to pass on the inside of the stone walls, from the roof to the cellar, where they were connected with terra-cotta pipes, laid under the cellar floor, and through these all the water was conveyed into the sewer on Thompson street. The separation between the Lecture Room and the Infant Sunday School Room was to be by sash, hung with weights and pulleys. A mistake on the part of the carpenter made them to swing on hinges. The committee, however, believing them to be satisfactory in this way, allowed them to remain the carpenter paying the difference in the cost. The space now occupied by the library room, together with the vestibule leading thereto, were, by the Architect's plan, intended to be a part of the Bible Class and Trustees' room. Believing that a room separated from the main room would be better for the Librarian's work, they had the plan changed to what it now is.

Three feet were also taken from the north end of the pastor's study, and made use of for closets and stationary wash-stand. A screen at the back of the centre block of pews, immediately in front of the main entrance door, was fixed by the committee to break the force of the air upon persons inside when the door was opened.

In addition to the regular contract made with Mr. Robt. Scott, there was a contract made with Morris and Haines, for three furnaces capable of warming the entire building, also for registers, dampers, &c.; the contract price for the work thus contemplated was $1,371, of which amount the furnaces cost $1,000. The back stairway leading from the Franklin street door up to the audience room, under the main contract, was only to be horsed up; the committee in view of the necessities which would frequently occur for its use, had it finished at a cost of $232. They had also seats put in the infant room for $167.50.

In addition to the items already specified as alterations or additions, the committee purchased the gas fixtures for $100, had a brick pavement laid on the north and east sides of the church, and had prepared the foundation for a slab pavement on Thompson and Franklin streets.

Everything which was needed to be done was done, in order that the congregation might be comfortable in their new place of worship.

These "extras" added a few thousands of dollars to the cost of the building, every cent of which is carefully recorded on the books of the treasurer.

In contemplating the work done thus far, we deem it our duty to place on record the conviction of all who have watched the progress of the building The contractor was a man with a conscience. He not only superintended the work, but worked himself. He was in earnest to make a good job. Living at Wilmington, Del., he felt that a church building of such proportions if substantially erected, would be to his advantage in securing contracts in this city. He slighted no place, and allowed no place to be slighted by his men, from the time the first stone was laid until the last nail under his contract was driven. Hence, we have full confidence in the *substantial* character of the building.

The building committee having an eye not simply to *beauty*, but to *strength* also, chose the style of architecture which the building has. They ignored the *high pitched roof*, preferring to increase the strength by *binding the walls together* with heavy girders.

All of the materials, whether of lime or stone, wood or iron, were ordered to be of the best quality. The lumber on reaching the ground was carefully inspected, and as agreed upon in the contract, not a board could be used which did not meet the approval of the committee.

All disputes arising between the commitee and the contractor, were to be referred to the Architect as umpire to decide. Happily very few matters had to be referred, as the contractor was seemingly bent on making our interests his own.

The opening of the "Lecture Room," was followed by a large increase in the congregation. This will readily appear when we mark the fact, that in the annual report made in January 1870, for a period covering the whole year, the basket collections amounted to only $113.33; while from the opening of the Lecture Room until January 1871, a period of less than eight months, the basket collections amounted to $390.47, a difference in favor of the shorter time of $277.14.

The pews, of which there were 96, rented quite as readily as was anticipated, and before the first six months had elapsed, all the most eligible had been taken.

The few who had been struggling to accomplish the work already done, soon found themselves encouraged and strengthened by fresh additions to their numbers. The coming together of the old and new, under God, did not partake so much of the nature of *adding*, as it did that of *blending*. We began to see not only new faces in our congregations, new names on our rolls, but new *workers* in our fields. We received fresh inspiration from new advisers, and fresh encouragement from new counsellors.

The moral strength received by new persons casting their lot with us, was fully appreciated by all the people. Among those who occupied official positions, it was frequently the theme of kindly remark, and we are not surprised that at the close of the year, several members of the Board of Trustees, resigned in order that their places might be filled by others who could officially bring their former experiences in other churches, to further the welfare of our own. The people heartily welcomed all who joined hands with them, and at the congregational meeting, January 9th, 1871, of the five trustees chosen, four were of those who had lately associated themselves with us, in the work of the Lord.

At this same congregational meeting, the Board of Trustees was authorized to create a mortgage on the church property, for such an amount as they thought necessary, not exceeding $25,000, the proceeds to be applied to the funding or cancellation of our present indebtedness.

Another matter of considerable importance was brought up at this meeting. It was an act authorizing the Board to issue stock or scrip, under the authority of this corporation, to an amount not exceeding $20,000, the proceeds to be applied to the completion of the church edifice.

After some discussion of this proposition, it was laid upon the table, to be taken up at an adjourned meeting of the congregation, on January 18th, 1871. The pastor was invited to be present at the adjourned meeting.

During the interval which elapsed between the stated and adjourned meetings, a conference was held by some of the male members of the church. At this conference the pastor brought forward the subject of the "Memorial Fund."

In 1869, when the two branches of the Presbyterian Church came together, there was a wide-spread enthusiasm throughout the whole church. The city of Pittsburg, where the Old and New School Assemblies merged into one, witnessed scenes memorable in the history of Presbyterianism. There was not only the procession, in which, by previous arrangement, former Old School men linked arms with former New School men, but there was also one of the grandest and most enthusiastic meetings ever held by a religious body. In the midst of this enthusiasm it was proposed by some members of the body to raise in the "Reunited Church" $5,000,000 as a "memorial" unto the Lord for his wonderful goodness and providence in bringing such a happy state of things to pass. This proposition was heralded throughout the land, and the church became committed to it.

When the General Assembly, after the reunion, met in the First Presbyterian Church in this city, in May, 1870, the proposition was brought forward, a committee appointed to see it carried out, and arrange all the machinery necessary to make it a success. Theological seminaries, colleges and professorships were to be endowed, and the work of the Lord generally was to be fostered and furthered by the munificent fund. The whole amount was to be raised by the time the Assembly met in 1871. The work was done, well done, and better done than the most sanguine had hoped for.

Certain churches like our own, engaged in building, were allowed to raise money to push forward their individual work, and for the amounts thus raised in the time specified, were to receive credit on account of the "Memorial Fund."

The brethren of the conference, upon learning

these facts, thought it best to waive all questions touching the issuing of stock or scrip, and see what they could do in the way of raising money, as authorized by the Memorial Committee. When, therefore, the congregation met, and had the Memorial Fund explained to them, they voted down the "resolution on stock or scrip," and appointed Messrs. S. Bradbury, Abner Lincoln, S. L. Kirk, Dr. B. C. Snowden, Dr. J. P. Curran, Lewis Davis, Robert Dornan, and Conrad B. Day, a Committee on Memorial Contributions." On motion, the pastor was added to the committee. This committee, as we find afterwards reported, succeeded in raising contributions to the amount of $10,293.75.

Soon after this, a mortgage of $25,000 upon the church property was negotiated with the Fire Association, and the mortgage of $7,500, given to Mr. Ellis, was paid off.

The congregation encouraged the Board of Trustees to go forward in the completion of the church building. With this in view, at their meeting, held May 8th, 1871, they unanimously elected Mr. Jacob Knight a member of the Building Committee.

The Building Committee invited proposals from several builders for the finishing of the church edifice. These proposals contemplated all the carpenter work, lumber, stairs, pews and plastering necessary for the completion of the work. The committee met at the office of the Architect, May 29th, 1871, to open these proposals, when it was found that the lowest estimate for the work was from A. Catnach & Son. A contract was entered into with them, and they commenced upon the work immediately.

A look at the church building at this time will not be out of place. All the stone work was done. The main entrance door on Thompson street, and the door on Franklin street, were finished and in place. All the windows on the lower floor were hung. On either side of the main door, as you entered, there was a temporary wall, of lathe, and one coat of plaster, so as to protect the Lecture Room from the rubbish which accumulated in the unfinished portion of the building. The two side entrances on Thompson street were boarded up, as were also the windows in the second story. The floor in the main room was laid, and the gallery joists in position. Within the walls, the Lecture Room and rooms adjoining were alone complete.

In view of a festival to be held in the church about this time, and as the work had to be done before the lathing and plastering commenced, the Building Committee engaged Mr. Hugh Thompson to introduce the gas-pipes. They also changed the original design, which was to have the gallery front circular, and arranged to have it straight. This change, and another, which provided a better pew end, brought the cost of the work contemplated by Catnach & Son to the sum of $10,000.

After due consideration, the Building Committee thought best to reduce the space allowed by the

Architect for the back stairway and pulpit recess. By cutting off three feet from this space, there was still left sufficient room for a wide stairway and pulpit recess; and while the architectural design was not interfered with, the audience room was increased in depth. This alteration was made by the contractors for $130. The plan of the Architect, upon which the contracter based his estimate, called for only 126 pews. There being ample room for more, the committee arranged to have 150. Afterwards, however, to allow a wider space between the pulpit platform and the pews in front of it, they had two taken out, leaving the number 148. In the gallery were placed eight very long pews.

The work of finishing now went forward quite briskly. The committee had other contracts to make, and they had to be continually on the alert, lest their delays might delay the work already advancing. Contracts were made with Mr. John Gibson to do all the frescoeing, after a design furnished by the Architect, for $770; with Messrs. J. and G. H. Gibson, to furnish, after approved patterns, all the glass required, for $1,455.57; with Mr. Charles M. Baker, to do all the painting, graining, oiling, &c., necessary to complete the church in the best manner, for $415; with Cornelius & Co., for furnishing gas fixtures and putting them up, for $400; and with Morris & Haines, for registers, &c., $148.

Looking forward to the completion of the church, which was expected about December 1st, 1871, it was thought advisable to have everything in complete readiness for dedication at that time. On Sabbath, July 9th, the pastor announced that a meeting of the congregation would be held on Wednesday, the 12th inst., to consider a matter connected with the opening of the church. At that meeting, the object was stated to be the appointment of a committee to make all arrangements for procuring a suitable organ to be used in the main audience room, now in process of completion. Whereupon Messrs. J. P. Curran, M.D., John Dickey, and Samuel H. Davis, were appointed. The distinctive title of the committee was, "The Organ Committee."

Soon after their appointment, they held a joint conference with the Building Committee. According to the Architect's plan, the organ was intended to be placed in the northeast corner of the building, alongside of the pulpit. At this conference, however, it was decided to place the organ in the gallery, and have the corner where it was originally intended to be, made to correspond with the other side of the pulpit, and to use the recess as a store-room.

Having decided as to where the organ should be placed, the Organ Committee began to inquire more particularly of what they were to do. They attended organ openings, corresponded with organ builders, studied the wants and wishes of the congregation, but concluded that for the present at least, they had better wait until other matters more important were attended to, and the finances of the church would

"THE NEW CHURCH"

warrant them in arranging for the building of such an organ as they believed the church needed. To bridge over from the present to a more favorable time, they hired an organ, which, with satisfaction, has been used until now.

Notwithstanding the expectations of the congregation, the work of finishing the church was not completed until the close of January, 1872. The dedication might have taken place in January had the committee forced the work along. They chose, however, to wait until everything was in complete readiness; until even the minutest matter had been attended to

On Thursday evening, February 1st, the Building Committee, with many of the members of the church, met in the audience room, to test the gas arrangements. The experiment proved that the style of lighting the church was satisfactory, both as to the softness of the light and the amount of light given.

When there was nothing further to be done, public notice was given, through the religious and secular papers, that the church would be dedicated to the worship of God on Sabbath, February 4th, 1872. A card similar to that which had been distributed at the time of the *opening* exercises in the Lecture Room, was printed, and copies sent to the friends of the church, and distributed throughout the community. This card contained the following programme of the "Dedication Services:"

Sabbath, February 4th, at 10½ A. M,

Sermon preached and Dedicatory Services conducted by the Pastor,

REV. JAMES Y. MITCHELL.

SERMONS BY

REV. R. H. ALLEN, D.D.,

At 3 P. M.

REV. H. C. McCOOK,

At 7½ P. M.

Monday, February 5th, 8 P. M.

UNION MEETING.

To be addressed by several neighboring pastors.

SERMONS.

Tuesday, February 6th, 8 P. M.

REV. J. L. WITHROW,

Pastor of Arch Street Presbyterian Church.

Wednesday, February 7th, 8 P. M.

REV. D. MARCH, D.D.,

Pastor of Clinton Street Presbyterian Church.

Thursday, February 8th, 8 P. M.

REV. E. R. BEADLE, D.D.,

Pastor of the Second Presbyterian Church.

Friday, February 9th, 8 P. M.

REV. H. JOHNSON, D.D.,
Pastor of First Presbyterian Church.

Sabbath, February 11th, at 10½ A. M.

Administration of the Sacrament of the Lord's Supper, by the Pastor.

3 P. M.,

Sunday School Jubilee.

ADDRESSES BY

REV. WM. O. JOHNSTONE,
Pastor of Kensington Presbyterian Church,
and the Pastor.

Singing and other exercises, by the Children of the Sabbath Schools.

7½ P. M.,

SERMON BY

REV. R. D. HARPER, D.D.,
Pastor of North Broad Street Presbyterian Church.

Monday, February 12th, 8 P. M.

Social Gathering and Selecting of Pews and Sittings.

This programme was fully carried out, except in two particulars. Rev. Dr. Beadle, having injured himself by a fall, was unable to be present. Rev. E. H. Nevin, D.D., pastor of the Reformed Church in Race street, below Fourth, took his place. Rev. Dr. Harper, could not attend, owing to sickness. The pastor occupied the pulpit in his stead. The Union meeting on Monday evening was participated in by Rev. W. T. Eva, pastor of Bethesda Church; Rev. Noah M. Price, pastor of Lutherbaum Church, and Rev. Wm. R. Work.

The weather during the services was very fine. We could hardly have looked for so mild a season during a winter month. Very large congregations attended the meetings, and a collection being taken up at each of the services, the treasury was benefited to the amount of $4,820.

A large number of persons attended the Social Gathering on Monday, February 12th.

The Board of Trustees had decided to sell the *choice* of pews. On the opening of the Lecture Room, the Trustees had acted on the principle that "the first coming should be first served." This arrangement did not give entire satisfaction. To avoid difficulty about location in the main room, they decided to sell the choice of pews at the time of the Social Gathering.

The purchaser did not acquire a *title* to the pew he selected, but simply the right to occupy it, subject to the rental as fixed by the Board of Trustees, and also to all regulations and restrictions which they from time to time might impose. The premiums for *choice* were made payable with the quarter's rent next due, and amounted to a few hundred dollars.

A committee of the Board—viz, S. L. Kirk, Jacob Knight, Robert Doman and Abner Lincoln, had previously prepared a schedule of the rentals, which was also approved by the Board.

At the time of the "sale of choice," the pews had tacked upon them, the amounts for which they rented, so that all choosing could do so intelligently. The renting of pews was as satisfactory as could be expected. The first annual report succeeding, showing a revenue from that source of over $5,000.

X.

AMENDMENTS TO THE CHARTER—INCREASING THE NUMBER OF MEMBERS IN THE BOARD OF TRUSTEES, AND CHANGING THE CHURCH NAME.

In the annual report of the Board of Trustees to the congregation, made at a meeting held January 8th, 1872, two very important propositions were brought forward. One of these contemplated a change in the "Corporate Title" of the church; the other "an increase in the number of the members of the Board of Trustees. These propositions had received the careful attention and consideration of the Board.

On Dec. 11th, 1871, they had appointed a committee "to consider the expediency of procuring an alteration in our church charter, changing our corporate name, and also increasing the number of trustees."

This committee at a meeting of the Board, held January 3d, 1872, reported as follows:

"That as our old name, 'the Trustees of the Central Presbyterian Church in the Northern Liberties,' has ceased to have any local significance attached to it, and is long and unwieldy; they recommend a change to the 'Grace Presbyterian Church of Philadelphia.'

They also recommend an increase in the number of members of the Board of Trustees from nine, the present number, to fifteen."

(Signed) S. L. Kirk, S. Bradbury, J. P. Curran, *Committee.*

When these propositions came before the congregation, the second was adopted at once, and with entire unanimity. The congregation had felt, that in a growing church, where so many were continually identifying themselves with us, that it was well to be more fully represented in the Board, so that the efficiency of the church might be increased, and her welfare promoted by additional counsellors.

The first proposition regarding the "change of name," did not at the time it was offered, meet with the same unanimous approval.

It was not to be wondered at that exceptions were taken to the action. Some believed that a change of name, would to some extent at least, destroy all previous history of the church.

Pleasant associations and happy religious hours, seemed to them to be in one way or another connected with the name, or at least the *name* linked *them* to these associations.

Others thought that a name worn with honor so long, ought not to be changed without some fuller explanation of the reasons for that change. It was true, the church was no longer in the "Northern Liberties," but there were other reasons, which to their minds were more potent and satisfactory, why it should be done; and these reasons ought to be embodied in some way, in any resolution which contemplated a change of name.

After some discussion of the subject, its further consideration was postponed, and the Trustees were directed to call a special meeting of the congregation at an early day, (giving two week's notice from the pulpit) to consider the question.

In the discussion of this subject, the Presbyteria reason for the change was mentioned, but not fully brought to the notice of the congregation.

After the "Reunion" of the two branches of the Presbyterian Church, the Presbyteries and Synods were reconstructed. Changes of names became not only frequent but necessary. The Fourth Presbytery, to which our church previously belonged, was incorporated with what is now the "Philadelphia Presbytery," and the Third Presbytery, with what is now the "Presbytery of Philadelphia Central."

In these changes, our own church being North of Market street, was by a geographical arrangement brought within the bounds of the "Presbytery of Philadelphia Central."

It so happened, that another church,(formerly Old School) the Central Presbyterian, was brought into the same connection. The sameness of name often produced great confusion in the public prints, and in Presbyterial and Synodical gatherings. It was felt desirable by many of the ministerial brethren, that either our own, or the other Central Church should accept the logic of events, and as many others had done, change the corporate title.

The other Church being our senior by a few years could not be expected to yield in this matter, so the question pressed itself upon us.

Many believed and do still believe, that the time is coming when there will be but *one Presbytery* to embrace all churches in the city. In such an event, another Central Church (colored) would be upon the roll, and add to the confusion of names.

Out of these facts, chiefly the whole discussion in our church was brought about.

The Trustees were in no immediate hurry to call another congregational meeting, preferring to wait until such times as they believed the whole matter would be well understood, and heartily acquiesced in by the congregation. In the meantime the members talked to one and another about it, and a conference of male members was held.

The Trustees seeing they must take steps to have the charter amended according to the vote of the congregation, touching an increase in the number of the Board; desiring to have but one expense and one trouble in bringing the charter for amendment before the court; and believing that they could no longer postpone the meeting, and comply with the directions of the congregation, which named "an early day," issued their call for a meeting to be held on Wednesday Evening, March 27th, 1872, immediately after the regular lecture.

The pastor without consuming the time usually taken up for lecture, retired to his study after the introductory exercises, to hold a conference with some of the ladies of the church, regarding the interests of the "Ladies Aid Society."

As soon as the congregational meeting had been organized, and the resolution under which it was convened had been read, Mr. W. R. Stewart moved "that a committee of conference, consisting of three persons, be appointed to prepare a preamble and resolution, and report to this meeting to night." The motion prevailed, and Messrs. W. R. Stewart, Abner Lincoln and W. L. Clifford, were nominated and elected the committee.

When the committee had retired, several of the members indulged in remarks on the subject. Presently the committee of conference returned and presented their report as follows:

"WHEREAS, the recent coming together of the two branches of the Presbyterian Church, has necessitated the blending of Presbyteries; and in many instances requiring new names to be given: and,

WHEREAS, in our own Presbytery thus united, there is another church organization known as the Central Presbyterian, which similarity of names causes much confusion in Presbyterial records; therefore,

Resolved, That while we cannot forget the past history of the church under the old name; and mindful of the ever watchful care of a kind Providence, who during a somewhat varied history has blessed and prospered us; we feel called upon as a concession to this spirit of union and harmony, so prominent in our united church, to change the corporate title; and be it therefore,

Resolved, That the Board of Trustees be authorized to take the necessary steps to so amend the charter, that hereafter the title of this corporation shall be ———— Presbyterian Church."

(Signed) WM. R. STEWART,
ABNER LINCOLN,
WM. L. CLIFFORD,
Committee.

On motion, the resolution attached to the report was adopted; after which the preamble in the report of the committee was adopted.

Messrs. J. P. Curran, M. D., Abner Lincoln and E. R. Craver, were appointed a committee to prepare a list of names to be voted for to fill the blank in the report of the committee. The name "Grace" as previously reported by the Board, was not presented at this meeting, because it was discovered that a Presbyterian mission had recently been started in the lower part of the city bearing the title.

The following names were presented to the congregation: Temple, Pisgah, Carmel and Emmanuel.

These names were voted for by ballot. The first ballot decided by a very large majority of all the votes cast in favor of the name "Temple." On motion the blank in the report of the committee of conference, was filled with the name "Temple," and the report as a whole was adopted without a dissenting voice.

When the congregation had finished the business which brought them together, and just before they had retired, the pastor returned to the Lecture Room from his study, and made a short address. He spoke of the circumstances which led to the consideration of the subject which had claimed their attention; of the former history and associations, which had clustered around the old name; of these being indestructible by any changes, whether of *location* or *name*; congratulated them on the name chosen; reminding them that the title was not only *distinctive*, but to his knowledge had never before been adopted by any church.

The Ancient Temple although costly and rich in ornaments, had a glory other than that found in its curious workmanship, and in its overlayings of gold and silver. Its main glory was in the extraordinary marks of the divine favor with which it was honored.

In it were the Ark of the Covenant, the Shechinah, the Urim and Thummim. As in the "Ark of the Covenant" were treasured the "*Tables of the Law*," so may this *Temple* hold with sacred reverence the laws of our God. As from the "*Mercy Seat*" which was upon the "Ark of the Covenant," the "Divine Oracles" were given out by an audible voice, so may we in this *Temple* hear the voice of God, in behalf of his people. As "The Shechinah" was visibly manifested by a *cloud* resting over the "Mercy Seat," so may we in this *Temple* have the *constant presence of God with us.* As by the "*Urim and Thummim*," God was consulted in all momentous and difficult matters, so may we by the word of God, and the ordiances appointed under God in this *Temple*, *hold counsel with Him* on all matters with which we have to do.

The glory of the "Second Temple" was greater than the former, *because Christ appeared in it.* May Christ not only appear, but abide with us. May the Holy Spirit ever manifest his wonderful work in enlightening and establishing God's children, and in quickening dead sinners into spiritual life; and when our works and services in this Temple are ended, may we all have a "*new name written on our foreheads*," and be permitted to join in the unending services of the "Heavenly Temple," with the blood-redeemed, who never weary in chanting with a loud voice, "Worthy is the Lamb, that was slain, to receive power, and riches, and wisdom, and strength, and honor, and glory, and blessing."

After this address the pastor led in prayer, and dismissed the congregation with the Apostolic Benediction.

The congregation having given the Board of Trustees authority to take such legal measures as were necessary to secure the amendments to the charter, the Board, at its meeting held April 8th, 1872, appointed Messrs. S. L. Kirk, Robert Dornan, and Lewis Davis, as a Committee for that purpose; this Committee engaged J. Austin Spencer, Esq., as Counsellor, and to him was committed the work of having the charter so amended as to conform to the vote of the congregation. It was not, however, until the meeting of the Board, held January 11th, 1873, that the committee were able to report their work done. On December 2d, 1872, the Court of Common Pleas, for the City and County of Philadelphia, after reciting that all proper legal steps had been taken in the matter, "did decree and declare, the name, style and title of this corporation to be changed to that of 'Temple Presbyterian Church;' also, that the Board of Trustees be increased in number from nine to fifteen members, allowing the election of five of these annually, on the second Monday in January, in each and every year, to serve for three years."

The first election under the amended charter, took place at the congregational meeting held January 13th, 1873.

The "Building Committee," after the dedication of the church, were continued by the Board; not because there was any work to be done for which they were specially appointed, but to attend to the collection of outstanding subscriptions, so far as they could, and pay off the indebtedness to contractors and others.

On December 9th, 1872, they made a final report of their operations to the Board of Trustees, which report was accepted, the Committee discharged, and the report adopted as a part of the annual report of the Board to the congregation. This final report of the "Building Committee," is a general outline of the work done from the time of its appointment, February 8th, 1869, up to the time of its discharge, December 9th, 1872, nearly four years, and was reported at the congregational meeting held January 13th, 1873.

A look at the building at this time, shows it completely finished within, in all its parts. Outside, a board pavement is laid, the Trustees hoping during the coming season, to be able to lay a flag pavement and put up an iron railing; when this is done, all is done which is needed for the accommodation, convenience and comfort of the congregation. The tower, according to the design of the architect, is intended to be finished out at the top with a spire. With this in view, all the necessary strength for such a purpose was maintained during the building of the tower, and all needed framework for the foundation of the spire was put in its place. This finish, not being absolutely needed, is not at the present time considered.

Looking over the past, we wonder how a church in a weakened condition, with but little financial ability, could ever have undertaken such a work as that, which we now call "finished." The secret of all is "Faith." The people believed in God. They believed that He who had cared for this church in days gone by, would care for it in the days of its trial and need. With faith they overcame doubts, and with faith they triumphed. Very generally too, they illustrated the truth of the text, from which the pastor preached his first sermon in the new "Lecture room:" "*For the people had a mind to work*," Neh. 4 ch. 6 v. Faith and works happily joined together, God owned and blessed. He gave them courage to endure until we entered into the new field. He then put it into the hearts of others to join hands with them. The body thus enlarged, was like-minded and like-determined—co-operation, sympathy, oneness, characterized it; and now we behold the results. While much remains to be done, may we not believe it will *soon* be done, after what we know has been done.

XI.

A LOOK AT THE SPIRITUAL CONDITION OF THE CHURCH.

The Church although so much engaged, and that too, from necessity, in things pertaining to her temporal interests, was not idle with regard to things spiritual. All the building operations, in which we were concerned, did not more interfere with us, than did the terrible feelings of suspense and doubt which pervaded the congregation, when it was generally believed that the *extinction* of the church was only a question of time.

At the time of the installation of Mr. Mitchell as pastor, the appearance of things was not very encouraging. The church had been without a pastor for more than a year. During that time, many of the people had attached themselves to other churches —the love of many had waxed cold—and some had ceased altogether to attend the ordinances of God's house. It was not to be supposed, that *all* the luke warm and indifferent, nor in fact that *any* of them would resume their places at the name of a *new pastor*, to them unknown and untried.

Nor could it be expected, that of those who had identified themselves with other churches, many of whom had been assigned to important offices therein, would relinquish their places and come back as before. The most that was looked for from these, was their *sympathy* and *good wishes*, (which had measurably been lost) and if circumstances required, their substantial support. These, under God, were in many instances secured.

At this time, there was but *one elder* in the church, Mr. William Sanderson, Sr. This fact weakened the hopes of the people; for as a church from its very commencement, until little more than a year of the time we now consider, it had prided itself upon a strong, efficient corps of men in the eldership.

There were less than 100 reliable names on the church register, when Mr. Mitchell was "*called.*"

At the congregational meeting which voted the call, there were but 61 votes cast. This, when it is remembered that special efforts were made to have a full meeting, that there was the excitement which always attends the choosing of a pastor, that *members of the church*, regardless of age, sex or pew rental, are permitted to vote for a pastor, shows no very encouraging numerical strength.

There were but 25 persons who held full pews, and 35 persons who held parts of pews or sittings, making a total of 60 persons, who contributed through the regular channel towards the support of the church.

From this showing, we could not expect to have large numbers in attendance upon the services of the church; prayer meetings and weekly lectures were considered well attended if there were 25 or 30 persons present.

The times themselves were unfavorable for any wide-spread religious influence. The "War for the

Union" absorbed the thoughts of the community. Every family almost, had a member in the ranks of our country's soldiery. There was great anxiety everywhere. There were daily expectations of some great battle, and news from "the seat of war" was eagerly sought after. It oftentimes appeared as though "war news" had been held back, or the march of armies had been so arranged, or the opposing forces had purposely begun their battles so as to have Sabbath days, days of peculiar excitement.

Many, if they did not get "war news" before they went to church, expected to hear "war sermons" in the church. The papers teemed with advertisements of "sermons to soldiers," or, "sermons in behalf of soldiers." Congregations anywhere and everywhere were incomplete unless made up in part of men in naval or military uniform. "Newsboys" shouted lustily their "extras" and "latest editions" hard by where congregations gathered; and it was no surprising thing, to see knots of people pouring over the contents of these papers in church vestibules.

The war encouraged excessive worldliness; money was easily to be made and people made it. Speculations became rife, investments were made in all kinds of stocks and securities, whether reliable or fancy, without the ordinary questioning and care which men are wont to exercise. It seemed as though people had abandoned themselves to think only of this world.

The frequent tidings of thousands killed in battle,

seemed to harden their hearts so that an allusion to death failed to move them. Such times were not favorable for making religious impressions.

God, during this time of war, seems to have reserved his special blessings for the men who had gone into the heat of battle. While the church mourned the coldness and worldliness of its members at home, there were frequent outpourings of the Holy Spirit upon those who had gone forth to war at the call of their country; and many who were strangers to God when they enlisted under our country's flag, became soldiers of the cross to fight under the flag of our King Emmanuel.

It is pleasing to note, that notwithstanding the unfavorableness of the times for extended religious effort, God never left the church without a witness. At the very first communion season in which Mr. Mitchell officiated, one came forward and united herself to the people of God. And at every communion succeeding, while we remained in the Old Church on Coates street, we had additional testimony that God was with us.

There were but two seasons of protracted services between 1862 and 1870.

Many of the few members we had, lived at long distances from the church, and it was quite impossible for them to attend with regularity the meetings. Some objected to coming, because of the rough characters and rough places in the neighborhood. It was thought best not to have *special* meetings, while the members thus excused themselves from attending.

The times when protracted services were held, seemed to be directed by God; and as a result of our waiting before Him, He gave us at our April communion in 1865, twelve, and at the April communion in 1868, twenty-three persons, to be added to the church on profession of faith. These two com munions furnished about one-third as many communicants as there were altogether on the roll in 1862.

During the other communions until the very last held in the Old Church, there were additions to our membership.

The last communion in Coates street, was held on *Sabbath evening, April 10th*, 1870. This being the *last time* for holding service in the Old Church, it was thought best to have the communion at that time, *instead* of the *morning*, as was the regular custom.

At this communion, two persons, one over seventy years of age, stood up and professed faith in Christ.

Looking over the whole period, seeing how the German character of the community did not warrant us in hoping for an increase in membership from it, remembering how " the war " engrossed the thoughts of all, how worldlymindedness ruled everywhere, how, when the war ended we had to consider and arrange for building elsewhere, it is a cause for congratulation and thanksgiving to God, that he not only kept our handful of people together, but during that time, (little more than seven years), gave witness, by additions to the church at every communion season, that He had not forsaken nor forgotten to remember us.

Upon entering our new building, the roll of members was made out anew with the following result:

Number enrolled as communicants . .	169
Of the 21 who organized the church there remained	3
Of those received during the ministry of Rev. Wm. H. Burroughs	2
Of those received during the ministry of Rev. A. Rood	21
Of those received during the ministry of Rev. J. P. Wilson, D. D.	8
Of those received during the ministry of Rev. G. W. Duffield, Jr.	54
Of those received during the ministry of Rev. James Y. Mitchell	81
Total	169

As arranged for in the programme of the opening exercises, there was a special communion season on the morning of the second Sabbath after we entered our "New Lecture Room."

It was hardly expected at that time, that any would profess their faith in Christ, but He who had remembered us at the last communion held in the Old Church, by putting it into the hearts of *two* to sit down for the first time at His table with His people, put it into the hearts of just double that number to join themselves to the people of God and sit down with them, when for the first time His table was spread in the New Church.

Besides these, five from sister churches, by certificate, cast in their lots with us at the same time.

From that time, we have had frequent manifestations of the Spirit of God being with us, and repeated assurances that He has owned and blessed the labors of His people.

In the Spring of 1871, there was a special religious interest pervading the congregation. An earnest desire prevailed for the salvation of souls. There was a greater wrestling with God in prayer. Additional meetings were demanded and held. These continued for four weeks ; quietness, depth of feeling, softening of hearts characterized them, and God gave us a testimony that He was pleased with us, by adding to the church on profession of faith, 33 persons.

Mr. Joseph F. Jaggers, formerly a member and elder in the Presbyterian Church at Fairton, New Jersey, having connected himself with this church, was elected a ruling elder September 28th, and installed the Sabbath following, October 2d, 1870.

The undivided attention of the people could not, nor can it yet, be given to the spiritual wants of the church.

When it is remembered that this was a period in which the work on the " Audience Room " was going on, and with it completed, provision must needs be made for all improvements on the outside of the building, also for the raising of funds to meet present indebtedness, surely the grace of God in Christ was manifested in bringing the hearts of His people to agonize over perishing sinners and to rejoice over sinners converted.

Up to the present time, we have had added to the church since locating in this new neighborhood, 195 persons.

Of the whole number of communicants on the roll since it was made out at the opening of the New Church, 13 have died, 5 have left because of removal from the city, and 11 have gone to sister churches nearer their present residences. With these losses, the church has yet a net increase to its roll, since May, 1870, of 166 members, making a total membership of 335.

Under the blessing of God during the past few years, notwithstanding the war and trials incident thereto, the apparent hopelessness of the cause, from a generally received impression that the church must die, the hardships connected with building a new church, and the forced division of thought between things temporal and things spiritual, the membership numerically was more than tripled, and the feeling of confidence and hope fully restored.

"The Lord has done great things for us, whereof we are glad."

Mindful of the past; remembering that God has

revealed a shining face from behind many a dark cloud; that he has led us safely through ways in which at first we feared to tread, we go on to our future work. Though much yet remains for us to do, we will trust in Him, who can make crooked places straight, believing that e're long all the claims against our church will be fully cancelled, and that this "Temple" will be filled with the songs of many, who, "new born," shall be further prepared and polished within these walls, for a place in the "Heavenly Temple" of our God.

THE SABBATH SCHOOL.

XII.

THE SABBATH SCHOOL.

No history of this church would, or could, be complete without an article on its Sunday Schools.

Prior to the *establishment* of this church, there were in operation Schools which became the objects of attention, care and oversight of this people as soon as they became distinctively a church organization.

Shortly after the installation of Rev. James Patterson as Pastor of the First Church, N. L., he secured the services of his people in gathering the neglected children of the district together, on the Sabbath, for the purpose of giving them *gratuitous* and *religious* instruction. As far as is known, this was the *first* school of the kind in this country.

This movement, so novel at that period, met with some opposition; but its success, after a time, won for it hosts of friends.

Under the teachings of their pastor, the membership of the First Church became largely engaged in the Sabbath School work. What was initiated with small beginnings grew into such large proportions, that in 1816 it was proposed to build a room capable of accommodating the crowds of children who sought Sunday School instruction. This occasioned the building of the "Old Lecture Room" on Coates street, west of Second, which was finished in 1818, and which stands until this day, although the encroachments of business have made it useless for the purpose for which it was originally intended.

The first members of our church were all recognized "Sunday School Workers," and they would have been degenerate children of a noble parentage had they been otherwise.

About the 1st of December, 1830, nearly five years before the organization of this church, about forty or fifty children were gathered together in the parlors of the house of Mr. Benjamin Naglee, then resident on Fourth street, below Green, and were formed into a Sunday School, with Mr. Naglee as Superintendent. In this place the Sessions were regularly held until the Spring of 1831, when the School was removed to Mr. John Dickerson's school-room, on Poplar street, above Second. This was about the time certain persons were dismissed from the First Church, and organized the Third Church, N. L. When the Third and Second Churches united under the name of the First Church, Penn Township, the school was transferred to the church building in Sixth street, above Green. When a portion of the members separated from that church, about fifty or sixty scholars accompanied them to the school-room on Poplar street. There they continued until April 19th, 1835, when they were removed to Commissioners' Hall, Third street, below Green, and from thence to the church building on Coates street, below Fourth, on November 14th of the same year.

From this we learn that our school had an existence prior to our distinctive church organization, and that its beginnings were characterized by the same vicissitudes as marked the beginnings of our church.

About one year after the school was established in the church building, it had increased so much in numbers, that it was divided into two departments, *male* and *female*.

The male department was under the charge of Mr. Benjamin Naglee, and the female under the charge of Miss Ann E. Reynolds. The former occupied what was afterwards known as the "Infant Sunday School Room," and the latter the "Session and Trustees' Room."

As part of the missionary labors among the young of the district, the First Church had established

Mission Schools" at different points. One of these was the "Eastburn School," so named out of regard to a minister of that name. This school was organized about the year 1825, and was situated on Charlotte street, between Beaver and George streets. During its existence it had as Superintendents, Messrs. Seth Collom and C. C. Aitken. The general average attendance was 120 scholars.

Another Mission School, established about the year 1827, was styled "The Nazarene." It was located, at the first, on Charlotte street, near Franklin (now Girard) avenue; afterwards, its location was changed to the north side of Franklin (Girard) avenue, between Third and Fourth streets. It had as Superintendents, Messrs. William Erhardt, Joseph Naglee, and Joseph Aitken. The average attendance was 80 scholars.

In October, 1837, the teachers of the church schools, and the teachers of the "Eastburn" (reported as the Fourth Street School), and "Nazarene" Schools, met together for the purpose of organizing what was afterwards known as "The Sabbath School Association of the Central Presbyterian Church of the Northern Liberties." On the 29th of October, 1837, these teachers adopted a constitution and by-laws; and on the 6th of November were fully organized under the same. The objects of the Association were set forth in the preamble, as follows:

"We, the undersigned persons, citizens of the Commonwealth of Pennsylvania, worshiping in the Central Presbyterian Church of the Northern Liberties, desirous of imitating our Lord and Master, Jesus Christ, who, when upon the earth, went about doing good, have formed ourselves into a society to give religious instruction to children on the Sabbath day, between the hours of divine service in the church, and, if need be, to search out those destitute of religious instruction, and convene them together in the Sabbath School, and, by our precept and example, aided by Divine grace, lead them to a saving knowledge of the truths contained in the Holy Bible."

This first Association was disbanded on June 2d, 1842; but on the very next day, another Association, with similar objects in view, and similar laws to govern it, was organized. From time to time, reorganizations have taken place, but up to the present time there exists "The Sabbath School Association." The direction of the school is under its control. By it all the officers in the Sabbath School are elected; and to it all reports of the work done in that special field are submitted. All the teachers and officers in the school, upon their election, and signing the constitution, are regarded in full membership.

THE MAIN SCHOOL.

At the first, all scholars were taught in the same room. Then there was the division into *male* and *female* departments. On March 7th, 1841, the larger scholars, of both these departments, were brought together in the Lecture Room (and formed what we denominate the "Main School"), under the superintendence of Mr. B. Naglee. This school has continued with varied success ever since. Up to the time of removal to our present location, the greatest number of scholars reported was in January, 1859, when the roll contained 257 names. The greatest number of teachers reported was 29, in November, 1858. At the time of the last report prior to our removal, there were 121 scholars enrolled, with an average attendance of 77. This number was considerably diminished when we first entered our new church, but at the present there are 210 scholars.

The school has also 7 officers and 35 teachers. Upon coming to the new church, the classes were designated by scriptural or other names, chosen by the teachers and scholars according to their own preferences, and associated with these names were appropriate mottoes.

BIBLE CLASSES.

While no definite information can be found upon the records concerning Bible Classes existing in the school during its earlier history, we know, by occasional references, that this part of the work was not overlooked. It would appear that at times the sexes were separated, and then again brought into the same class together. The first recorded information on the subject is concerning a class organized June 16th, 1861, by Mr. S. L. Kirk. At first it numbered 2 male and 7 female scholars. The whole number afterwards increased to 22. On March 19th, 1866, the class was divided, and two classes, one male, and the other female, were formed; the first under the charge of Mr. Morris Ebert, and the other under the charge of Mr. D. C. Golden. At the present time there are five Bible Classes, two male, and three female—numbering in all 55 scholars.

INFANT SCHOOL.

On March 7th, 1841, the Infant School was organized. The primary object was to educate the "little ones" sufficiently to enable them to take their places in the classes of the "Main School." This school is still in active operation. A superintendent and three assistants, by various methods, teach them to recite passages of Scripture, answers to questions in Catechism, and such hymns as are easily understood by the young. From this school there are transferred from time to time, into the Main School, scholars who are advanced sufficiently to read and understand the Bible. The school now numbers 200 scholars.

MISSION SCHOOLS.

The "Nazarene," which came under the control of the Association when it was first organized, continued in existence until May 7th, 1840, when it was discontinued as a separate school, because the building in which it was held had to be taken down at the time of the widening of Girard avenue. At that time it was united with the Eastburn, or Fourth Street School.

The Fourth Street School ceased to make reports to the Association, from May 7th, 1840; and, from the silence of the records, we judge it had no connection with the Association from that time.

A Mission School was organized about the year 1841, at the northwest corner of Tenth and Coates streets. It had 7 teachers and 35 scholars.

A Mission School was organized February 11th, 1857, in Poplar street, above Fifth. Mr. Wm. Sanderson, Sr., was the superintendent, and he was assisted by a corps of twelve teachers. The number of scholars increased from 40 to 110. This school was discontinued May 9th, 1858. It was merged into a Mission School, which at that time was established in the American Mechanics' Hall, at the corner of Fourth and George streets. This school was at different times under the direction of Messrs. G. C. Bower, Wm. Sanderson, Sr., and C. C. Aitken. It had upon its roll 26 teachers and 355 scholars. After an existence of three years and four months, it was removed to the church in July, 1861.

The "Allen Street School" was taken in charge January, 1859. Mr. C. C. Aitkin was superintendent, and the average attendance of scholars about 85. The room in which the school was held had to be vacated, and it being impossible to secure another suitable in the neighborhood, the school was disbanded in November of the same year.

On September 21st, 1868, a communication from Mr. I. M. Price, superintendent of the "Union Mission School," at the southwest corner of Ninth and Girard Avenue, was received, asking that his school be brought into connection with our "Association." The school had a library, singing and text books, five teachers and about forty scholars. It having been stated that Mr. B. D. Stewart had agreed to pay the rent of the hall, and that it was desirable in view of our proposed removal to that neighborhood to commence Sunday School operations there, the "Union Mission School" was taken under our jurisdiction, and the teacher's names enrolled as members of the "Association." This school was merged into the church school as soon as it was transferred to the new building. At the present time we have no school operations outside of our church. Since occupying this field we have districted the neighborhood, appointed visiting committees to canvass it and procure new scholars, and have tried to have the school all that its warmest friends could desire. The number of scholars at present enrolled, is 470.

MONTHLY PRAYER MEETING.

In April, 1857, the "Association" adopted a resolution, providing for the holding of a prayer meeting on the first Sabbath afternoon in every month, at the close of the regular Sabbath School exercises. This time was afterwards named by the "Association," as "Missionary Afternoon." With occasional interruptions a prayer meeting has been held on that afternoon since its appointment, and God has often blessed it in the way of encouraging the teachers, strengthening their faith and converting the scholars.

LIBRARY.

We have not been able to discover when and to what extent a library was first introduced into the Sabbath School. Knowing, however, that it was deemed an essential part of a well ordered school in the parent Presbyterian Church of the Northern Liberties, as early as 1827, we may conclude it was provided for at the very beginning of our school operations. The first report which we have upon the subject, July 5th, 1842, mentions 514 books upon the catalogue, but only 311 fit for use. At the present time the books are all equal to new in appearance and condition, and number 850 volumes.

SUNDAY SCHOOL PAPERS.

In the year 1849, "The Youth's Penny Gazette," a Sunday School paper, was introduced into the school, and from that time until the present, some paper, previously agreed upon by the "Association," has been distributed at least monthly among the scholars. At the present time, the larger scholars receive "The Presbyterian Sabbath School Visitor," published by our own "Board," and the infant scholars, "Morning Light," published by the "American Tract Society."

REWARDS.

The system of rewards was introduced into the school, in September, 1840. To encourage the scholars in punctuality, good behaviour, committing to memory verses of scripture, or recitations in the catechism, they were promised tickets of *red* or *blue*, which had printed upon them a verse or verses of scripture. A value was fixed on these tickets, (one of red being equal to ten of blue), and they were given to the scholars according to their conduct or attainments, as measured by a standard determined upon by the "Association."

When a scholar secured a number of these tickets, upon returning them, he was entitled to a book, worth as much as the tickets, to which also a *money* value had been given. This method of rewarding the scholars continued with occasional variations, until we entered our new church.

A system of merit tickets (or merit certificates) has since been adopted. On the face of these certificates is marked their value—*one*, *five* or *ten*. The scholars receive these, according as they deserve them, for "*bringing in new scholars ; punctuality ; regularity ; recitations in Scriptures, Catechism, &c.*" A certain number of ten merit tickets entitle the holder to have his name placed on "The Roll of Honor," or to have a "badge" marked "Diligent," "Faithful," "Excellent," or "Distinguished," as the case may be. Other rewards follow for continuance in well-doing; such as the reception of Bibles or other books; and classes which have attained distinction receive, on anniversary day, class banners appropriately marked. The Session of the church also encourages the scholars in the study of the Shorter Catechism, by giving to such as may commit it to memory a copy of the Bible.

The rewarding of scholars for work done during the year is a pleasing feature of our anniversary day, which is observed on or about the 1st of May in every year.

MISSIONARY SPIRIT.

In June, 1839, there was formed what was denominated "The Sabbath School Juvenile Missionary Society." The object of this society was to excite and increase a missionary spirit among the children. This society, as such, has passed out of existence, but the objects and aims for which it was formed are remembered and cherished. Looking over the records, we learn that at one time the contributions are for a "library," to be sent to the Cherokee Mission; at another, they are designed for the education of young men in Constantinople. Now they go to a needy school in New York; now to one nearer home; now to a French, and now to an Indian missionary. Now to the home field, and now to the foreign field. Other objects than those distinctively missionary are remembered. Money, at one time, is raised and given for the soldiers' orphans at Gettysburg; at another, for the sufferers by the fire at Chicago. The whole field for Christian labor and Christian sympathy is kept in view, and the children, by monthly or by special contributions, do something for the general cause of missions, or give their support to some specified object.

To support the school, the scholars and teachers contribute monthly to what is known as the "Sunday School Fund." The money received from this source is not sufficient for the purpose intended. It has always been the effort of the Association to have the school perfect in its arrangements and appointments. The contributions in the school, over and above what goes to missionary and special purposes, are not large enough to meet the requirements of a school in these days. Hence we have an annual collection in the church, on or about the third Sabbath in December. This is the only opportunity the congregation has during the year to give to the Sabbath School cause. About the time of this collection, the school receives a legacy of $50 from the estate of Mr. Benjamin Naglee, its first superintendent. To supplement these collections, necessity has compelled the Association to hold, at different times, concerts, exhibitions, &c., in order to meet the demands upon its treasury. In these several ways the school has not only been maintained free from debt, but enabled to do a work for others beyond its own sphere.

Under the direction of Mr. Lewis Davis, Librarian, the Library Room in the new church was fitted up at an expense of $110, and the money paid from the library fund. The table in that room was presented by Mr. Geo. D. B. Kelly, 409 Brown street.

The school became interested in the work of building the new church, and gave over and above their other contributions towards its completion. Not only do we find the "young people" credited with an amount towards the "construction fund," but mention also is made of special objects.

"Calvary Bible Class" gave the window which bears its motto, "In Christ's Death we have our Life;" also, the Oxford edition of the Bible, which is on the pulpit.

"Naomi Class" gave the window which bears its motto, "May Christ make our Lives *Beautiful;*" also, the table on which to place the baptismal bowl.

"Cross-Bearers' Bible Class" had the communion service renovated, and "Lilies of the Valley" Class furnished the marker for the pulpit Bible; while both joined with the rest of the classes in giving the windows bearing the mottoes, "Here the Cross; Hereafter the Crown;" "Jesus gives Grace and Glory."

The school has often been visited by the Holy Spirit, with his convicting and converting power. Many of its scholars have become active members of the church; and as its numbers increase, we look for a corresponding increase in the membership of the church.

We regard the Sunday School work of the church as the most important which claims our attention. Hence we have labored in it, and encouraged others to labor. We have been blessed with a faithful corps of teachers, and we have no doubt that many will hereafter call them blessed.

"*He that goeth forth and weepeth, bearing precious seed, shall doubtless come again with rejoicing, bringing his sheaves with him.*"

THE LADIES' AID SOCIETY.

XIII.

"THE LADIES' AID SOCIETY."

While it is conceded that the male members of every church and congregation should direct its affairs, it is a question whether there ever was a church building begun, and successfully carried forward to completion, without the help of ladies.

As at the first, women brought bracelets, and earrings, and jewels of gold, for the building of the Tabernacle; so, until the last, when a house is to be built unto the Lord, we will find *women* earnestly engaged therein.

We Presbyterians are not easily carried away with the popular clamor of the day, about "Woman's Rights;" but in view of what our ladies have done for the church, we concede it as a "right" that their work should be historically recorded.

In the early history of our church, we find occasional allusions to "The Mite Society." No definite information is given of its organization, or the extent of its work. All we know is, that it was under the control of the ladies, and the object in view was to relieve the corporation of its financial troubles.

In Jannary, 1851, there was a vote of thanks tendered by the Board of Trustees to the ladies, for the "liberal and handsome donation of $100 towards defraying the expenses incurred in carpeting the church," after certain alterations had been made.

At other times, when the congregation was greatly embarrassed, we see mention made of certain ladies who came forward and gave liberally towards its relief.

As early as the year 1866, when the subject of our removal to another locality began to be agitated, the ladies, without waiting for an organization to be perfected, made arrangements for the holding of a "Fair."

Without exception, all cheerfully engaged in the work. Many, at their own homes, made useful and fancy articles; many interested their friends, in and out of the city, to work for them. Times were fixed when, as a body, they met at each other's houses to labor and consult together, and provide for the successful carrying on of the enterprise.

When all things were in readiness, the Fair was commenced, and continued for several days, in December, 1866, at the Hall southwest corner of Ninth and Spring Garden streets. When it closed there, it was with the understanding that it should be continued at some other time in the Lecture Room of the church. Here it was opened in June, 1867, and continued for several days.

There being no immediate demand for the money thus secured, it was invested in Government bonds, until the Fall of 1868, when it was paid over to the Board of Trustees as part of what was needed to purchase our present church site.

This contribution from the ladies was $1,166.81, *and was the first available money the church had when it determined to move.*

In June, 1869, in order to systematize their work, they met at the house of Mrs. Hannah Naglee, and organized "The Mite Society." Officers were chosen, and twenty-four managers were appointed. The special duty of these managers was to secure a small voluntary contribution, *monthly*, from every member of the church, or from such friends of the church as felt disposed to give. Being formed into an organized society, the ladies were better enabled to adopt other methods for securing funds. They fixed as the special object of their labors, "the furnishing of the new church."

Under the auspices of this society, it was determined to give a "Supper." Again, it was arranged to give the supper in the new church building. We dare say that never did ladies so generally and so energetically engage in any undertaking. Evening after evening they met, and planned, and prepared to provide satisfactorily for a large number of persons; and evenings of planning and preparation were followed by days of "ticket selling."

February 17th, 1870, was the time fixed upon for the supper. When that evening arrived, the crowd which filled the building gave evidence that the ladies had done their work well. It was estimated that at least one thousand persons sat down at the tables, and there was a clear gain to the treasury of the "Mite Society," by this effort, of $807.02.

After coming to the new church, other ladies who joined our congregation became interested in the work, and in November, 1870, a Fair was held for some days in the main audience room, which was still in an unfinished condition. At the close of the Fair, a supper was given. With the same energy which characterized the former effort, the ladies engaged in this, and increased their treasury $1,375.00.

In January, 1871, the name of the organization was changed; and with occasional changes in officers and managers since, it now exists under the title of "The Ladies' Aid Society." Not omitting to collect monthly from subscribers, the Society, since its formation, has adopted, from time to time, other expedients to raise means to carry forward the work contemplated. Festivals, Tea Drinkings, Select Readings, Public and Parlor Concerts, have been resorted to; and from these various sources more than $6,000 have been raised.

While the ladies have contributed to the Construction Fund of the church, they have kept in view the object they proposed at the beginning, viz.: "the furnishing of the church;" and as a matter of interest, as well as of information, since that work is one, we itemize the disbursements:

LECTURE ROOM.

For Upholstering, - - - - -	$333.99
" Matting, and putting it down, -	221.11
" Pulpit carpets, - - - -	56.80
Total, - - - - -	$611.90

In addition to this, they received as donations:

From I. H. Wisler, 12 chairs.
" Wm. R. Stewart, mirror for pastor's study.
" Wm. Hogg, Jr., carpets for study and class-room.
" Wm. Sanderson, Sr., furniture for pastor's study.

MAIN AUDIENCE ROOM.

Pulpit furniture, - - - - -	$647.00
Carpets, - - - - -	968.00
Matting in vestibules, &c., - - -	403.82
Upholstering, - - - - -	1,251.69
Total, - - - -	$3,270.51

They received also as donations:

From Allen & Brother, the boquet table in the pulpit, and
" R. Dornan, the pulpit mat.

This showing is surely gratifying; and may we not believe that they who have already accomplished so much, with continued determination will accomplish still more? Many of the ladies have, as individuals, been generous contributors, but their *joined hands* enabled them to do a work of which we all are justly proud.

A CLOSING THOUGHT.

A review of the period since you and I were brought together, as pastor and people, compels to grateful thanksgiving.

It is now more than eleven years since, for the first time, I occupied your pulpit. It is fast approaching that time, since, by Presbyterial action, we were joined in our present relation.

Those years have been fraught with wonder in the world. Not to speak of the overturnings beyond the seas, we have witnessed the wonder workings of the Lord Omnipotent in our own land. Through the fires of war, our country has received a new baptism. There have been wonders in the church at large, and our own denomination has been surprisingly wrought upon.

No longer does one say, "I am *Old School*," and another, "I am *New School*," but, without prefix or affix, we delight, *in Union*, to say, "We are Presby terians."

The preceding pages tell the story of our individual church.

When we think of the past, and look on the present, in wonderment we ask, "What hath God wrought?"

Since we first were wedded in this church relation, I have wept with you, and you have wept with me, over loved ones, snatched from the arms of our earthly affection, and together, in our sorrow, have we gone and told Jesus.

The church in heaven is more brilliant, because of those we gave it from our church on earth.

Upon the heads of many, either in infant days or adult years, have I sprinkled the waters of baptism, and to many have I given the hand of fellowship, as, for the first time, they came to the table of the Lord.

It is pleasing to think that nothing has transpired to break the peace which should ever be between pastor and people.

To *your kindness*, *forbearance* and *charity*, under God, I must attribute the unbroken harmony which has been, and which, I trust, will continue to be.

Considering the infirmities of our nature, the weaknesses and misunderstandings of life, it is a cause of thankfulness to God that he has kept us together as *one.*

Building a church is the rock on which many a congregation has split. Yet under great difficulties we began, continued, and for more than a year have worshipped in the building finished and dedicated, and the congregation is intact.

To the praise of God let it be written, that during the whole of our building operations there was no jarring and no break in our harmony. While, because of our *manhood*, there were differences of opinion, there were no disturbances. There was bearing as well as forbearing; and at any time, from the commencement of the work until its close, could I have raised my hands over the congregation and said, "How sweet and how pleasant it is for you, brethren, to dwell together in unity." So MAY IT ALWAYS BE SAID.

Let us labor and serve together, waiting for the Master's call, when from the church militant we shall rise to the Church Triumphant; where no fear will ever be, of mistakes, misconceptions and misunderstandings, but where, in unbroken unity, we will serve God forever and forever.

ORDER OF EXERCISES;

TOGETHER WITH THE

FORM USED

BY THE PASTOR,

AT THE

DEDICATION

OF THE

NEW CHURCH,

N. E. CORNER OF

Franklin and Thompson Streets,

FEBRUARY 4th, 1872.

ORDER OF EXERCISES.

Invocation by the Pastor.

SINGING THE HYMN.

Before Jehovah's awful throne,
Ye nations bow with sacred joy;
Know that the Lord is God alone,
He can create, and he destroy.

His sov'reign power, without our aid,
Made us of clay, and form'd us men;
And when like wand'ring sheep we stray'd,
He brought us to his fold again.

We'll crowd thy gates with thankful songs,
High as the heavens our voices raise;
And earth, with her ten thousand tongues,
Shall fill thy courts with sounding praise.

Wide as the world is thy command;
Vast as eternity thy love;
Firm as a rock thy truth shall stand,
When rolling years shall cease to move.

Reading the 48th Psalm.

By Rev. B. B. Parsons, D.D.

Prayer,

By Rev. William Speer, D.D.

SINGING THE HYMN,

All hail the power of Jesus' name!
Let angels prostrate fall;
Bring forth the royal diadem,
And crown him Lord of all.

Sermon,

By the Pastor, Rev. Jas. Y. Mitchell.

Text—"What hath God wrought?"—Numbers, xxiii. 23.

COLLECTION.

Dedicatory Exercises.

---

* The singing was by the *congregation*, and was led by the Precentor, Wm. H. Moyer, and the Organist, Mrs. Eliza McKinley.

FORM USED AT THE DEDICATION.*

[After the sermon and collection, the pastor requested the Elders, Trustees, and heads of families, to come forward and arrange themselves in front of the pulpit, and the other members of the congregation to rise in their places.]

The pastor then said:

According to the notice publicly given, we have assembled to day to dedicate this house to the worship of the only living and true God—Jehovah, Father, Son, and Holy Ghost. Now, if it is your desire that we should proceed to this service, let the Elders and the Trustees, together with all the members of the congregation, declare unto us, and say:

Have you been moved to the erection of this edifice by a sincere desire to continue among you the regular and solemn worship of the Most High God, for the spiritual benefit of yourselves and your families, and of this community?

Answer.—We have.

Is it your desire, and your solemn purpose, that this edifice shall be a house of worship, and devoted sacredly to the ordinances of religion, according to

* From the Presbyterian Manual.

the customs and order of the Presbyterian Church in these United States?

Answer.—It is.

Do you now, with one heart, give up this house to God, the Father, the Son, and the Holy Ghost, to be henceforth a house of prayer, a temple to his praise; and do you promise to provide for and to maintain here religious worship, seeing to it that nothing shall be wanting that may be needful for the decency, and propriety, and convenience thereof, according to the customs and order, as aforesaid, of the Presbyterian Church?

Answer.—We do.

Blessed be the Lord God, who hath put it into your hearts to build this house unto his name. The Lord accept the labor of your hands, which you have offered unto him this day, and make good to you, and to your children after you, the word which he hath spoken. "In all places where I record my name, I will come unto thee, and I will bless thee."

Let us pray.

PRAYER*.

Holy, holy, holy Lord God Almighty, which is, and was, and is to come. The whole earth is full of

* From the "Book of Public Prayer," compiled from the authorized formularies of worship of the Presbyterian Church, as prepared by the Reformers, Calvin, Knox, and others.

Thy glory! Thine, O Lord, is the greatness, and the power, and the glory, and the victory, and the majesty; for all that is in the heaven and in the earth are Thine. Now, therefore, we thank Thee, O God, and praise Thy glorious Name.

But who are we, that we should be able to offer so willingly after this sort? For all things come of Thee, and of Thine own do we give Thee? O Lord our God, all this store that we have prepared, to build Thee an house for Thy holy name, cometh of Thy hand, as is all Thine own.

Now behold, O Lord our God, and look unto this place where we are gathered in Thy name, and have respect to the prayer of Thy servants, and to their supplication, to hearken unto the cry and the prayer that Thy servants pray before Thee this day, to take for Thine own this house which we would give Thee.

O Lord God, who art from everlasting, and whose kingdom is without end, Maker of heaven and earth and sea, and all that in them is; King of Kings and Lord of Lords, Lawgiver, Defender, and Judge alone, to Thee we dedicate it.

Holy and blessed Trinity, Father, Son and Holy Ghost, three Persons in one God, to Thee we dedicate it.

Father of all who believe in Jesus, and God and Father of our Lord Jesus Christ, here meet Thou with Thy children; teach them, strengthen them, and bless them. To Thee we dedicate it.

Son of God, the only begotten of the Father, Head over all things, the Lord our Righteousness, Saviour, Shepherd, High Priest, and Advocate, here draw all men unto Thee; here sprinkle Thy ransomed ones with Thine atoning blood; here make Thy flock to lie down in green pastures, beside the living waters; here be Thou a shadow from the heat and a refuge from the tempest; and while Thy people worship in the outer sanctuary, pray for them within the Holiest of all. To Thee we dedicate it.

Holy Ghost, proceeding from the Father and the Son, who didst come down upon our Lord Jesus beside Jordan, and upon the Church at the Pentecost. Who takest up thine abode in all believers; Comforter, Inspirer, Sanctifier, here display Thy power, succeed Thy truth, give hope to the penitent and gladness to the mourner; subdue Thy foes, hallow Thy Church, and accomplish all the glory of redemption. To Thee we dedicate it.

Arise, O Lord, into Thy rest, Thou and the ark of Thy strength.

But will God in very deed dwell with men on

the earth? Behold, the heaven and heaven of heavens cannot contain Thee; how much less this house which we have builded? Yet dwellest Thou also with him that is of a contrite and humble spirit. So be Thine eyes opened toward this house night and day; and toward the place of which Thou hast said, My Name shall be there: and hearken Thou unto the supplication of Thy servants, and of Thy people Israel, when they shall pray toward this place; and hear Thou in heaven, thy dwelling-place; and when Thou hearest, forgive. Dwell thou with us in Thy temple, while we are yet in the world; then take us up to Thy house in heaven, that we may dwell with Thee forever.

Give ear, O Shepherd of Israel; Thou that leadest Joseph like a flock; Thou that dwellest between the Cherubim, shine forth.

How dreadful is this place! This is none other but the house of God, and this is the gate of heaven!

After prayer, the congregation sang the hymn:—

I love thy kingdom, Lord,
The house of thine abode,
The church our blest Redeemer bought
With his own precious blood.

I love thy church, O God!
  Her walls before thee stand,
Dear as the apple of thine eye,
  And graven on thy hand.

For her my tears shall fall,
  For her my prayers ascend;
To her my cares and toils be given,
  Till toils and cares shall end.

Beyond my highest joy,
  I prize her heavenly ways,
Her sweet communion, solemn vows,
  Her hymns of love and praise.

Jesus, thou Friend divine,
  Our Saviour and our King,
Thy hand from every snare and foe
  Shall great deliverance bring.

Sure as thy truth shall last,
  To Zion shall be given
The brightest glories earth can yield,
  And brighter bliss of heaven.

This was followed by singing the Doxology:

Praise God from whom all blessings flow;
Praise him all creatures here below;
Praise him above, ye heavenly host—
Praise Father, Son and Holy Ghost.

After which the congregation was dismissed with the Apostolic Benediction by the pastor.

DIRECTORY.

"LET ALL THINGS BE DONE DECENTLY AND IN ORDER."

1 Cor.: xiv. 40.

CHURCH DIRECTORY.

RECEPTION OF NEW MEMBERS.

Persons are received into the membership of this church *at any time*, by bringing certificates of dismission from other churches, or passing a satisfactory examination on experimental piety, before the Session of this church.

The *public reception* of new members takes place on *Communion Sabbaths*, and immediately before the administration of the Sacrament of the Lord's Supper.

FORM OF RECEPTION.

[The pastor having stated, that at a meeting of the Session, the following persons were received into the membership of the church on profession of their faith, shall proceed to call their names. Those answering to the names shall come from their seats and arrange themselves in front of the pulpit. While they continue standing, the pastor shall address them as follows:]

In the presence of your Maker, and of this assembly, you do now appear, desiring, publicly and solemnly, to enter into covenant with God and with this church, according to the Gospel; professing your full assent to the following summary of faith:

1. You solemnly and publicly profess your belief in one God, the Almighty, Maker of heaven and earth, who upholds all things, and orders all events, according to his own pleasure, and for his own glory. Deut. vi. 4. Rev. iv. 11. Jer. x. 10. 1 Cor. viii. 4, 6.

2. You believe that this glorious Being exists in three persons—God the Father, God the Son, and God the Holy Spirit; and these three are one, being the same in substance, equal in power and glory. John i. 1, 14. Acts v. 3, 4. 1 John v. 7.

3. You believe that the Scriptures of the Old and New Testaments are given by inspiration of God, and are our only rule of faith and practice. 2 Tim. iii. 16. Isaiah viii. 20. 2 Peter i. 19, 20, 21. Gal. i. 8, 9.

4. You believe that God at first created man upright, in the image of God; that our first parents

fell from their original uprightness, and involved themselves and their posterity in a state of sin and misery. Gen. i. 27. Rom. v. 12. Eph. iv. 24.

5. You believe that all men, since the fall, are by nature depraved, having no conformity of heart to God, and being destitute of all moral excellence. Gen. vi. 5. Ps. xiv. 2, 3. Rom. iii. 10, 18.

6. You believe that Jesus Christ is the Saviour of sinners, and the only Mediator between God and man. Matt. ix. 13. 1 Tim. ii. 5.

7. You believe in the necessity of the renewing and sanctifying operations of the Holy Spirit, and that to be happy you must be holy. John iii. 3, 5. Titus iii. 5.

8. You believe that sinners are justified by faith alone, through the atoning sacrifice of Jesus Christ. Eph. ii. 8. Rom. iii. 24.

9. You believe that the saints will be kept by the mighty power of God, from the dominion of sin, and from final condemnation, and at the last day they will be raised incorruptible, and be forever happy with the Lord. John x. 27, 28, 29. Job xix. 26, 27. 1 Cor. xv. 51, 54.

10. You believe the finally impenitent will be punished with everlasting destruction from the

presence of the Lord, and from the glory of his power. Rev. xxii. 15. Matt. xxv. 46.

Thus you believe in your heart, and thus you confess before men.

[Here the pastor, descending from the pulpit, baptizes those who have not previously been baptized. Returning to the pulpit, he addresses all as follows:—]

You do now, under this belief of the Christian religion, as held in this church, publicly and solemnly avouch the Eternal Jehovah, Father, Son and Holy Ghost, to be your God and the God of yours; engaging to devote yourselves to his fear and service, to walk in his ways, and to keep his commandments. With an humble reliance on his Spirit, you engage to live answerably to the profession you now make, submitting yourselves to the laws of Christ's kingdom, and to that discipline which he has appointed to be administered in his church. That you may obtain the assistance you need, you engage diligently to attend, and carefully to improve, all the ordinances he has instituted.

Thus you covenant, promise and engage, in the fear of God, and by the help of his Spirit.

[The pastor now announces the names of those who have been received by certificate from other churches, together with the names of the churches from which they have been received. As these names are called, the persons answering to them rise up in their places.]

The pastor then requests all the members of the church to rise and sing:—

Praise God from whom all blessings flow;
Praise him all creatures here below;
Praise him above, ye heavenly host;
Praise Father, Son and Holy Ghost.

[After the singing, the pastor says:—]

In consequence of your *professions* and *promises*, and *by reason of your coming to us from s ster churches*, we affectionately receive you as members of this church, and in the name of Christ declare you entitled to all its visible privileges.

We welcome you to this fellowship with us in the blessings of the gospel, and on our part engage to watch over you, and to seek your edification, as long as you shall continue among us. Should you have occasion to remove, it will be your duty to seek, and ours to grant, a recommendation to another church; for hereafter you cannot withdraw from the watch and communion of the saints without a breach of covenant.

The people here join in singing:

Blest be the tie that binds
  Our hearts in Christian love;
The fellowship of kindred minds
  Is like to that above.

Before our Father's throne
  We pour our ardent prayers;
Our fears, our hopes, our aims, are one;
  Our comforts and our cares.

We share our mutual woes,
  Our mutual burdens bear;
And often for each other flows
  The sympathizing tear.

When we asunder part,
  It gives us inward pain:
But we shall still be joined in heart,
  And hope to meet again.

[After the singing, the pastor concludes these exercises with the following benediction:]

May the Lord support and guide you through a transitory life; and, after this warfare is accomplished, receive you all to that blessed church, where our love shall be forever perfect, and our joy forever full. Amen.

BAPTISM OF CHILDREN.

While, for good and sufficient reasons, parents may have their children baptized at home, the nature of the sacrament itself, and the new and peculiar relations to the church into which children are brought by its administration, make it desirable that, as a rule, children should be baptized publicly, in the presence of the church.

Parents may have their children baptized on any Sabbath, provided they have given notice to the pastor, or some member of the Session, some time previous to the day on which they desire the sacrament to be administered.

The established custom of this church is, for the pastor to announce from the pulpit, at least two weeks before the time, that parents having children unbaptized are requested to bring them forward for baptism on the approaching Communion Sabbath.

Parents should consider it their *duty* to furnish the pastor with the names of their children, dates when they were born, and the parents' names, prior to the administration of the sacrament, in order that they may be recorded in the church books.

FORM USED AT THE BAPTISM OF CHILDREN.

[When the sacramental season has arrived, at the time designated in the "ORDER OF WORSHIP FOR COMMUNION SABBATHS." the pastor shall make a brief address touching the nature and design of the sacrament.]

[After the address, the congregation shall sing a hymn appropriate to the occasion.]

[During the singing of the last verse of the hymn, the parents, bringing their unbaptized children with them, come forward and stand in front of the pulpit.]

When the singing is concluded, the pastor shall say:—

Baptism was instituted by the Lord Jesus Christ, the great Head of the Church, to be a seal of the covenant of grace, and the ordinance of admission to a visible standing in his church.

The water in this ordinance implies guilt and pollution, and represents to us justification by the blood of Christ, and regeneration and sanctification by his Spirit.

But you are not to conclude that this, or any outward ordinance whatever, will be sufficient for the salvation of the soul.

It is the blood of Christ alone that cleanseth from all sin; and to this you are exhorted ever to look for your own salvation and that of your children.

If it should please God to spare your lives, and the lives of your children, until they come to years capable of receiving instruction, it will be your duty to teach them, or cause them to be taught, to read God's holy word; to instruct them in the great principles of the Christian religion; to pray for them and with them; to set an example of piety and godliness before them; and, by all the means of God's appointment, to bring them up in the nurture and admonition of the Lord.

These duties, and whatever you are convinced, or shall be convinced, from the Word of God, to be binding on you as Christian parents, you do promise and covenant, in the presence of God and his church, that, as He shall give you strength, you will endeavor to perform and do.

[Upon the conclusion of this address, and after the parents have covenanted to perform the duties enjoined, the whole congregation shall rise, and be led in prayer by the pastor, for the parents and children, thus solemnly brought before them.]

THE CHILDREN SHALL NOW BE BAPTIZED.

[After the baptism, the pastor shall again lead the congregation in prayer, remembering not only those already mentioned, but all the baptized children of the church, together with their parents.]

This prayer concludes the solemn and impressive service.

THE LORD'S SUPPER.

The seasons of sacramental communion occur in the morning of the second Sabbath in the months of January, April, July, and October.

A lecture, or sermon, preparatory to the Communion season, is delivered on the Friday evening next preceding each Sacramental Sabbath.

No trifling excuse should prevent any member of the church from attending this service.

ORDER OF WORSHIP

For Sabbath Mornings and Evenings.

INVOCATION.*

Concluding with the Lord's Prayer.

Singing.

Reading the Scriptures.

Prayer.†

Singing.

COLLECTION.

Reading Pulpit Notices.

Sermon.

Prayer.

Singing.

(*The congregation standing.*)

BENEDICTION.

---

* The Invocation is omitted in the evening.

† The congregation stands during prayer.

ORDER OF WORSHIP

For Communion Sabbaths.

INVOCATION.

Baptism of Children.

Singing.

Prayer.

Singing.

Collection for the Sessional and Poor Funds of the Church.

Reading Pulpit Notices.

Reading the Scriptures.

Sacramental Address.

Invitation to Visiting Christians to Commune with us.

Reception of New Members.

Singing the Hymn:

'Twas on that dark and doleful night,
  When powers of earth and hell arose
Against the Son of God's delight,
  And friends betrayed him to his foes.

Before the mournful scene began,
He took the bread, and blessed, and brake;
What love through all his actions ran!
What wondrous words of grace he spake!

"This is my body, broke for sin,
Receive and eat the living food;"
Then took the cup and blessed the wine—
"'Tis the new covenant of my blood."

"Do this," he cried, "till time shall end;
In memory of your dying Friend,
Meet at my table and record
The love of your departed Lord,"

Jesus, thy feast we celebrate,
We show thy death, we sing thy name,
Till thou return, and we shall eat
The marriage supper of the Lamb.

[During the singing of this hymn, the pastor and elders take their seats in front of the congregation, and near the communion table.]

Administration of the Sacrament.

Singing.

BENEDICTION.

WEEKLY MEETINGS.

There is a stated weekly Lecture on Wednesday evening, in the Lecture Room.

A weekly Congregational Prayer Meeting is held on Friday evening, in the Lecture Room.

The Sabbath School meets every Sabbath afternoon. Unless by direction of the Sabbath School Association, its meetings are ordered to be held on Sabbath mornings during the warm months of summer.

MONTHLY MEETINGS.

The Board of Trustees meets on the second Monday night in every month.

The Sabbath School Association meets on the fourth Monday night in every month.

MEETINGS OF SESSION.

The first Monday night in every month, is the time for the monthly meeting of the Session.

Frequent meetings of the Session are held previous to every Communion Season, of which due notice is given from the pulpit on the Sabbath preceding.

Certificates of Dismission to other churches are granted by the Session of the church. Application for them should be made at least one week before the time they are required. No certificate will be granted to a person who is in arrears for pew rent or other money obligation to the church, unless the Session is satisfied that the arrearage is unavoidable, and the reason given will be perfectly satisfactory to the Board of Trustees.

ANNUAL MEETING.

The annual meeting of the congregation, for the election of Trustees, and the transaction of other business appertaining to the temporal interests of the church, is held on the second Monday night of January in each year.

FORMER ELDERS.

BENJAMIN NAGLEE,	Deceased.
CHARLES ELLIOT,	"
JOHN A. STEWART,	"
ISAAC ASHMEAD,	"
WM. T. DONALDSON,	"
SAMUEL T. BODINE,	Elder now in the Second Presbyterian Church, Germantown.
B. D. STEWART,	Elder now in the North Broad St. Presbyterian Church.
WM. SANDERSON,	Elder now in the Woodland Presbyterian Church.
H. H. SHILLINGFORD,	Elder now in Spring Garden Presbyterian Church.
GEORGE C. BOWER,	Ceased to act.
JAMES NEELY,	Bethesda Presbyterian Church.

PRESENT ELDERS.

JOSEPH AITKEN, ABNER LINCOLN,
JOSEPH F. JAGGERS.

THE BOARD OF TRUSTEES.

The list here given shows the regular succession in the Board of Trustees from the time the charter was granted until the present time.

The dates indicate the time of the election. All elections by the congregation were, and still are, for three years, unless it is specially named that the person was elected in the place of one resigned, when the election was for an unexpired term.

Where there is a *, it shows that the election was by the Board of Trustees, and the person so elected was to fill the unexpired term of the one resigning.

TRUSTEES UNDER THE CHARTER.

To serve until the second Monday in January, 1837.

Benjamin Naglee, Charles Elliot,
John A. Setwart.

To serve until the second Monday in January, 1838.

Edward Patteson, Casper Yeager,
Peter Mintzer.

To serve until the second Monday in January, 1839.

Joseph Pond, Joseph Naglee,
John G. Flegel.

ELECTIONS UNDER THE CHARTER.

January 9th, 1837.

Benjamin Naglee, Charles Elliot,
John A. Stewart.

January 8th, 1838.

Wm. P. Aitken, John T. Smith,
Charles C. Aitken.
Edward Patteson, *vice* Joseph Naglee, resigned.

January 16th, 1839.

Joseph Pond, John G. Flegel,
Edward Patteson.

January 14th, 1840.

Samuel T. Bodine, John A. Warner.
Wm. A. McKee.
*John A. Stewart, *vice* John G. Flegel, resigned.

January 11th, 1841.

Wm. T. Donaldson, Elihu D. Tarr,
Wm. P. Aitken.

January 10th, 1842.

Joseph Pond, Wm. Sanderson,
Edward Patteson.

January 17th, 1842.

*Benedict D. Stewart, *vice* Joseph Pond, resigned.

January 16th, 1843.

James Morrell, Samuel Grice,
G. C. Bower.
C. B. Dungan, *vice* Edward Patteson, resigned.

January 26th, 1843.

*S. T. Bodine, *vice* James Morrell, resigned.

February 28th, 1843.

*John T. Smith, *vice* S. T. Bodine, resigned.

June 6th, 1843.

*J. G. Flegel, *vice* C. B. Dungan, resigned.

January 8th, 1844.

Edward Patteson, S. T. Bodine,
Thomas Beaver.
James Morrell, *vice* J. T. Smith, resigned.

April 13th, 1844.

*Jonathan Leidigh, *vice* B. D. Stewart, resigned.

January 13*th*, 1845.

George W. Morse, Wm. A. McKee,
Augustus H. Raiguel.

January 12*th*, 1846.

James Morrell, James Taylor,
Thomas Potter.

January 11*th*, 1847.

Joseph Aitken, Henry Davis,
William Sanderson.

Budd S. Bodine, *vice* James Taylor, resigned.
Robert M. Foust, *vice* Geo. W. Morse, "

August 11*th*, 1847.

*Thomas Beaver, *vice* B. S. Bodine, resigned.

October 9*th*, 1847.

*B. D. Stewart, *vice* R. M. Foust, resigned.

January 11*th*, 1848.

Benedict D. Stewart, William A. McKee,
William P. Eckhardt.

January 8*th*, 1849.

John T. Smith, Thomas Beaver,
Robert M. Foust.

February 10th, 1849.

*Elihu D. Tarr, *vice* John T. Smith, resigned.

January 14th, 1850.

Joseph Aitken, Augustus H. Raiguel,
Henry Davis.

Wm. Sanderson, *vice* Wm. A. McKee, resigned.

April 13th, 1850.

A. H. Campbell, *vice* Thomas Beaver, resigned.

January 13th, 1851.

B. D. Stewart, William Sanderson,
G. C. Bower.

September 14th, 1851.

*Wm. B. Elliot, *vice* A. H. Raiguel, resigned.

January 12th, 1852.

*A. H. Campbell, R. M. Foust,
Cyrus C. Moore.

January 10th, 1853.

J. Austin Spencer, William F. Smith,
H. H. Shillingford.

October 15th, 1853.

*John Snyder, *vice* A. H. Campbell, resigned.

January 9th, 1854.

B. D. Stewart, H. Davis,
John T. Smith.

Edward Patteson, *vice* Wm. F. Smith, resigned.
Joseph Aitken, *vice* C. C. Moore, "

January 8th, 1855.

John Snyder, Samuel B. Grice,
William B. Elliot.

January 14th, 1856.

S. T. Bodino, William Sanderson,
Edward Patteson.

January 26th, 1857.

John T. Smith, Thomas Cunningham,
B. D. Stewart.

January 11th, 1858.

G. C. Bower, H. H. Shillingford,
John Snyder.

May 10th, 1858.

*Wm. Seeley, *vice* John Snyder, resigned.
* Samuel Grice, *vice* H. H. Shillingford, res'd.

October 11th, 1858.

*Benj. C. Naglee, *vice* Samuel B. Grice, res'd.

February 9th, 1859.

Edward Patteson, William Sanderson,
S. L. Kirk.
R. S. Bower, *vice* J. T. Smith, resigned.

January 9th, 1860.

Robert Aitken, George W. Hart,
William M. Weckerly.

January 14th, 1861.

William Seeley, William B. Elliot,
William R. Bald.
Geo. W. Grice, *vice* Edward Patteson, resigned.

February 11th, 1861.

*Samuel Bradbury, *vice* S. L. Kirk, resigned.

January 13th, 1862.

William Sanderson, James M. Lamon,
Abner Lincoln.
Samuel Bradbury, *vice* Wm. M. Weckerly, res'd.

January 12th, 1863.

Robert Aitken, S. L. Kirk,
Samuel Bradbury.

January 11th, 1864.

William Seeley, William R. Bald,
William R. Stewart.

October 10th, 1864.

*Wm. B. Elliot, *vice* Wm. R. Stewart, res'd.

January 9th, 1865.

William Sanderson, Abner Lincoln,
James M. Lamon.

January 8th, 1866.

S. Bradbury, R. Aitken.
S. L. Kirk.
D. C. Golden, *vice* Wm. B. Elliot, resigned.

January 14th, 1867.

William R. Bald, William R. Stewart,
Ansel Collins.
Wm. Seely, *vice* Wm. Sanderson, resigned.
D. C. Golden, *vice* James M. Lamon, resigned.

January 13th, 1868.

William Seely, A. Lincoln,
D. C. Golden.

November 9th, 1868.

*Joseph F. Jaggers, *vice* D. C. Golden, resigned.

January 27th, 1869.

S. L. Kirk, Robert Aitken,
S. Bradbury.

January 10th, 1870.

Lewis Davis, J. H. Workman,
William R. Bald.

January 9th, 1871.

Jacob Knight, J. P. Curran, M. D.,
Abner Lincoln.

Robert Dornan, *vice* J. H. Workman, resigned.
B. C. Snowden, M. D., *vice* Robert Aitken, "

January 8th, 1872.

Samuel Bradbury, S. L. Kirk,
Conrad B. Day.

January 13th, 1873.

Samuel H. Davis, Robert Dornan,
Lewis Davis.

In addition to the above, at this meeting there were elected under the amended Charter (which provided for 15 persons in the Board, instead of 9) the following persons:

John Dickey, I. H. Wisler,	To serve for 3 years.
Isaiah Davis, Wm. M. Cramp,	To serve for 2 years.
W. S. Wilson, T. W. Wolf.	To serve for 1 year.

April 14th, 1873.

*Wm. R. Stewart, *vice* S. Bradbury, resigned.
*Joseph W. Golden, *vice* W. S. Wilson, resigned.

May 12th, 1873.

Robert Aitken, *vice* John Dickey, resigned.

PRESENT ORGANIZATION OF THE BOARD OF TRUSTEES.

President,
ABNER LINCOLN.

Secretary,
LEWIS DAVIS.

Treasurer,
S. L. KIRK.

Pew Agent,
ISAIAH DAVIS.

Jacob Knight,
Conrad B. Day,
Robert Dornan,
I. H. Wisler,
T. W. Wolf,
J. P. Curran, M. D.,
Samuel H. Davis,
William M. Cramp,
Joseph W. Golden,
Robert Aitken,
William R. Stewart.

FORMER SUPERINTENDENTS OF THE MAIN SUNDAY SCHOOL.

Benjamin Naglee,
C. B. Dungan,
Wm. T. Donaldson,
B. D. Stewart,
David McClure,
E. M. Gregory,
D. C. Golden,
Robert Aitken,
Edward Patteson,
William A. McKee,
Thomas Potter,
Isaac Ashmead,
Joseph Aitken,
George W. Grice,
S. L. Kirk,
S. H. Jenkins.

FORMER SUPERINTENDENTS OF THE INFANT SCHOOL.

Ann E. Reynolds,
Mrs. J. W. Wilson,
Lizzie W. Hall.

PRESENT ORGANIZATION OF THE SUNDAY SCHOOL ASSOCIATION.

President,

D. C. Golden.

Vice President,

Abner Lincoln.

Secretary,

Wm. P. White.

Treasurer,

Robert Aitken.

Main School Superintendent,

James Y. Mitchell.

Assistant Superintendent,

Wm. M. Clark.

Secretaries,

Thomas Gillam, William S. Golden.

Librarian,

William P. White.

Assistants,

Frank P. Webb, George H. Barrow.

Teachers.

Tillie Snyder,
Flora E. Lincoln,
Maggie Solliday,
Hannah Davis,
Laura Curran,
Carrie Grim,
Hannah Golden,
Beckie McManes,
Sallie M. Horn,
Ella Ely,
J. L. Saxton,
Wm. R. Stewart,
S. L. Kirk,
George W. Golden,
Theo. R. White,
W. M. Read,
Lewis Davis,
Rosa Fronefield,
Fanny Fay,
Mattie Jaggers,
Addie Ely,
Susan McFarland,
Mary S. Rainier,
Lillie R. Aitken,
Jennie V. Davis,
Sallie Shaw,
Annie Kirk,
Haddie E. Gray,
Robert Aitken,
A. Lincoln,
T. W. Wolf,
Thomas Summerville,
Joseph Aitken,
William A. Bosler,
Theo. F. Read.

Superintendent of the Infant School,
JOSEPH W. GOLDEN.

Assistants.

SADIE E. CAMPBELL,
ANNIE C. SKINNER,
ELLA G. GRAEFF.

NAMES OF THOSE WHO HAVE BEEN SEXTONS IN THIS CHURCH.

[The date indicates the time when their services began.]

Appointed by the Association.

Nicholas Helverson.

Elected by the Board of Trustees.

B. Vickery, - - -	September 20th, 1836.
Budd S. Bodine, - -	January 26th, 1843.
George Adams, - -	December 16th, 1844.
George Beecher, - -	May 19th, 1845.
D. Richardson, - -	October 19th, 1846.
George Beecher, - -	May 8th, 1847.
Enoch Mayhew, - -	June 12th, 1847.
James Crawford, - -	October 8th, 1855.
John Springer, - -	October 1st, 1862.

CONSTITUTION AND BY-LAWS.

CONSTITUTION

OF

THE CENTRAL PRESBYTERIAN CHURCH,

IN THE

NORTHERN LIBERTIES, PHILADELPHIA.

PREAMBLE.

We, the subscribers, citizens of the Commonwealth of Pennsylvania, and members of the Society of Presbyterians of the said church, worshipping God in the new church on Coates street, between Third and Fourth streets, in the Northern Liberties aforesaid, having some time since associated as a congregation for religious purposes, and being desirous to acquire and enjoy the powers and immunities of a corporation or body politic in law, have adopted the following constitution:

ARTICLE I.

The name style and title of the Society shall be, "The Trustees of the Central Presbyterian Church in the Northern Liberties, Philadelphia."

Article II.

The affairs of the said corporation shall be conducted by nine Trustees, three of whom shall be elected annually on the second Monday in January in each and every year hereafter, to serve for three years, or until others are elected; of which election notice shall be given in the church on the previous Sabbath. But in case it should happen that an elec tion of Trustees should not be made as aforesaid, the corporation shall not for that cause be deemed to be dissolved; and it shall be lawful, on any day within sixty days thereafter, notice having been given as aforesaid, to hold and make an election of Trustees as aforesaid. And in case of any Trustee's death, resignation or removal, his place may be filled for the remainder of his term in such manner as the ordinances or by-laws of the said Trustees shall for that purpose direct.

Article III.

The present Trustees of the said Society shall continue in office as follows, to wit: Benjamin Naglee, Charles Elliot, and John A. Stewart, until the second Monday in January, Anno Domini 1837; Edward Patteson, Casper Yeager, and Peter Mintzer, until the second Monday in January, Anno Domini 1838;

and Joseph Pond, Joseph Naglee, and John G. Flegel, until the second Monday in January, Anno Domini 1839, or until others shall be elected as aforesaid.

Article IV.

The officers of the Board of Trustees shall consist of a President, Secretary and Treasurer. The Treasurer may be elected from among the members of the Society who are not members of the Board of Trustees—all of whom shall be citizens of Pennsylvania.

Article V.

The qualifications of both the electors and Trustees of the said society shall be, that such persons shall have been members of the Society for six months at least previous to such election; and shall have paid six months' rent for a pew or part of a pew within the said church, and shall not be in arrears for more than one years' rent at the time of such election, and be of the age of twenty-one years or upwards, and citizens of this Commonwealth.

Article VI.

The said corporation shall not engage in any way not authorized by the ordinary usage and practice of said Society, whereby the said society may or shall, on any one occasion, be involved in an expense of three hundred dollars or upwards, without having obtained the concurrence of at least seven of the Trustees.

ARTICLE VII.

The clear rents and profits of the real estate of the said Society, and the interest and dividends of their money, stock, and other personal estate, shall not exceed two thousand dollars per annum.

ARTICLE VIII.

By-laws not repugnant to the Constitution and laws of the United States, to the Constitution and laws of this Commonwealth, or to this instrument, may be passed by a majority of the said Trustees at any meeting.

BENJAMIN NAGLEE, PETER MINTZER,
CHARLES ELLIOT, JOSEPH POND,
JOHN A. STEWART, JOSEPH NAGLEE,
EDWARD PATTESON, JOHN G. FLEGEL,
CASPER YEAGER.

PHILADELPHIA, FEBRUARY, 1836.

To the Supreme Court of the
Commonwealth of Pennsylvania.

I, James Todd, Attorney General of the Commonwealth of Pennsylvania, do hereby certify, that I have perused and examined the above written instrument, and am of opinion that the objects, articles and conditions therein set forth and contained, are lawful.

In witness whereof, I have hereunto set my hand, at Philadelphia, the sixteenth day of March, Anno Domini 1836. JAMES TODD.

To His Excellency, the Governor
of the Commonwealth of Pennsylvania.

We, the Justices of the Supreme Court of the Commonwealth of Pennsylvania, certify that having perused and examined the above written instrument, concur in opinion with the Attorney General, that the objects, articles and conditions therein set forth and contained, are lawful.

Witness our hands, at Philadelphia, the twenty-third day of April, Anno Domini 1836.

JOHN B. GIBSON,
MOLTON C. ROGERS,
JOHN KENNEDY.

I, Henry Witmer, Prothonotary of the Supreme Court of the Eastern District of Pennsylvania, do hereby certify, that the above written instrument or Charter of Incorporation, was duly presented to the Justices of the Supreme Court of the Commonwealth of Pennsylvania, agreeably to the rule of Court in such cases made and provided, and by them duly allowed, as in their certificate set forth.

In testimony whereof, I have hereunto set my hand, and affixed the seal of the said court, at Philadelphia, this twenty-fifth day of April, Anno Domini 1836.

[SEAL.] HENRY WITMER.

PENNSYLVANIA, SS.

In the name and by the authority of the Commonwealth of Pennsylvania, Joseph Ritner, Governor of the said Commonwealth, to Thomas H. Burrowes, Esquire, Secretary of the said Commonwealth, sends greeting:

[SEAL.] Whereas, it has been duly certified to me, by James Todd, Attorney General of the said Commonwealth, and by John B. Gibson, Esq., Chief Justice, Molton C. Rogers and John Kennedy, Associate Justices of the Supreme Court of Pennsylvania, that they have respectively perused and examined the above act or instrument for the incorporation of "The Trustees of the Central Presbyterian Church in the Northern Liberties, Philadelphia," and that they concur in opinion that the objects, articles and conditions therein set forth and contained are lawful; Now, know you, that in pursuance of an act of the General Assembly, passed the sixth day of April, in the year of our Lord one thousand seven hundred and ninety-one, entitled "An act to confer on certain associations of the citizens of this Commonwealth the powers and immunities of corporations or bodies politic in law;" and a supplement to the same, passed the eighth day of April, in the year of our Lord one thousand eight hundred and thirty-three, I have transmitted the said act or instrument of incorporation unto you, the said Thomas H. Burrowes, Secretary of the said Commonwealth hereby requiring you to enroll the same, at the expense of the applicant, to the intent that, according to the objects, articles and conditions therein set forth and contained, the parties may become and be a corporation and body politic in law and in fact, to have continuance by the name, style and title in the said instrument provided and declared.

Given under my hand and the great seal of the State, at Harrisburg, this eighth day of July, in the year of our Lord one thousand eight hundred and thirty-six, and of the Commonwealth the sixty-first.

By the Governor.

THOMAS H. BURROWES,
Secretary of the Commonwealth.

Commonwealth of Pennsylvania,
Secretary's Office.

Enrolled in Charter Book No. 6, page 15, containing a record of acts incorporating sundry literary, charitable and religious institutions.

[SEAL.] Witness my hand and seal of office, at Harrisburg, this eighth day of July, in the year of our Lord one thousand eight hundred and thirty-six, and of the Common wealth the sixty-first.

THOMAS H. BURROWES,
Secretary of the Commonwealth.

AMENDMENT OF ARTICLE VI.

Agreeably to a vote of the congregation, given January 20th, 1851, the following amendment to the 6th Article of the Constitution was presented to a Court of Common Pleas, held January 30, 1852:

Article VI.

"That the Board of Trustees shall not have power to purchase or sell any real estate, or to incumber any real estate already vested in the corporation, or to incur any liability exceeding in amount the sum of three hundred dollars, unless a resolution authorizing such purchase, sale or incumbrance shall have been first submitted to the congregation, at the regular annual meeting thereof, or at a special meeting duly convened for that purpose, when a vote of a majority of the members present shall be necessary to pass such resolution; excepting in all cases the current expenses of the corporation."

On motion of J. Austin Spencer, Esq., the Court ordered that the said instrument be filed, and that notice of the said application be published according to law.

On the 3d day of March, 1852, due proof having been exhibited of said publication, and the Court having examined the said instrument of writing, and the objects, articles and conditions therein contained appearing to be lawful, and no cause being shown to the contrary, did decree and declare, that "the same shall be deemed and taken to be a part of the instrument upon which the said corporation was formed and established, to all intents and purposes, as if the same had originally been made part thereof; and further, did direct that the said alteration or amendment shall be recorded in the Office for Recording deeds, &c., for the City and County of Philadelphia."

The amendment was recorded in the Office for Recording of Deeds, &c., for the City and County of Philadelphia, March 8th, 1852, in Miscellaneous Book, G W C, No. 1, page 350.

AMENDMENTS OF ARTICLES I. AND II.

Agreeably to the votes of the congregation, given at meetings held January 8th and March 28th, 1872, the following change of name, amendments and alterations to Articles I. and II. of the Constitution were presented to the Court of Common Pleas for the City and County of Philadelphia, to wit:

That Articles I. and II. be amended so as to read as follows:

Article I.

That the name style and title of the Society shall be, "Temple Presbyterian Church."

Article II

The affairs of the said corporation shall be conducted by fifteen Trustees; five of whom shall be elected annually on the second Monday in January in each and every year hereafter, to serve for three years, or until others are elected, of which election notice shall be given in the church on the previous Sabbath. But in case it should happen that an election of Trustees should not be made as aforesaid, the corporation shall not for that cause be deemed to be dissolved; and it shall be lawful, on any day within sixty days thereafter, notice having been given as aforesaid, to hold and make an election of Trustees as aforesaid. *Provided, however*, That the six additional Trustees required by this amendment shall be elected at the election in January, 1873, two of them to serve for one year, two of them for two, and two for three years. And in case of any Trustee's death, resignation or removal, his place shall be filled for the remainder of his term in such manner as the ordinances or by-laws of said Trustees shall direct."

The Court heard the petitioners on November 8th, 1872, when, on motion of J. Austin Spencer, Esq., the Court ordered the instrument to be filed, and that notice of said application be published according to law.

On December 2d, 1872, due proof having been exhibited of such publication, and it appearing that notice of the intended change of name had been given to the Auditor General, and the Court having examined the said instrument of writing, and the objects, articles and conditions therein contained appearing to be lawful, and no cause being shown to the contrary, did decree and declare, "that the name, style and title of said corporation be changed to that of "Temple Presbyterian Church;" that the first and second Articles of the Charter of Incorporation, of the said corporation, shall be altered and amended, according as the same is herein specified and set forth; so that the same shall be deemed and taken to be part of the instrument upon which the said corporation was formed and established to all intents and purposes, as if the same had originally been made part thereof. And did further direct and decree, that the said alteration and amendment be recorded in the Office for the Recording of Deeds, &c., for the City and County of Philadelphia."

Recorded in the Office for the Recording of Deeds, &c., for the City and County of Philadelphia, in Miscellaneous Book F T W, No. 1, page 67.

BY-LAWS

OF

THE BOARD OF TRUSTEES.

ADOPTED MAY 12, 1873.

ARTICLE I.

Meetings.

SEC. 1. The Stated Meetings of the Board shall be held as follows: One for the organization of the new Board, within ten days after the election, and on the second Monday evening of each month in the year. The hour of meeting shall be, from April till September, at 8 o'clock; and September to April, 7½ o'clock. Eight members shall constitute a quorum to transact business.

SEC. 2. Special Meetings shall be called by the President, at the written request of five members; the object of the meeting shall be stated in the notices to be issued by the Secretary.

SEC. 3. No business shall be transacted at a Special Meeting, except that for which such meeting is specially called.

ARTICLE II.

Order of Business.

1. Prayer.
2. Roll Call.
3. Reading of Minutes.
4. Reports of Officers.
5. Reports of Committees.
6. Unfinished Business.
7. New Business.

ARTICLE III.

Officers of the Board.

SEC. 1. The Officers of the Board shall be a President, Secretary, Treasurer, and Pew Agent, who shall be elected by ballot annually, and continue in office until their successors are elected.

SEC. 2. The President (or, in his absence, the President *pro tem.*) shall preside at all meetings of the Board. He shall have the custody of the Charter of the church, sign all orders drawn upon the Treasurer and attested by the Secretary, appoint all committees not otherwise ordered, and perform the duties usually appertaining to his office.

SEC. 3. The Secretary shall keep regular and correct minutes of the proceedings of the Board; notify them, in writing, of the time and place of meetings; attest all orders drawn upon the Treasurer; take charge of the seal and papers belonging to the corporation; furnish the chairman of each committee with a list of its members, and perform the usual duties of a Secretary.

SEC. 4. The Treasurer shall have charge and keep a correct account of the funds of the Corporation; pay no moneys but on orders properly attested, except the Pastor, Sexton, Choristers and Organist's salaries, and gas bills as they become due. He shall report the condition of the Treasury, monthly, and present to the Board, annually, in January, a statement of the receipts and expenditures for the past year, the same to be read before the corporation at their annual meeting. He shall deliver to his successors all moneys and papers in his possession belonging to the Corporation.

SEC. 5. The Pew Agent shall take charge of the Pew Books, rent pews and sittings, keep a correct account of all moneys collected, and pay the same to the Treasurer forthwith, taking his receipt therefor. He shall make quarterly reports to the Board of the amount collected, and also of delinquent Pew Renters, and the annual value of the pews rented.

ARTICLE IV.

Pew Rents.

SEC. 1. The pew rents shall be paid quarterly in advance, on the first day of January, April, July and October; and it shall be the duty of the Pew Agent to attend in the church to receive the pew rents, notice of such sitting having been previously read from the pulpit.

SEC. 2. When any person shall become indebted for three-quarters pew rent, the Pew Committee may place the same in the hands of a collector, and the cost of collection shall be added to the pew rent.

ARTICLE V.

Standing Committees.

SEC. 1. The Standing Committees of the Board shall be appointed annually, at the first Stated Meeting after the election of Trustees, and shall consist as follows:

SEC. 2. A Committee on Real Estate, consisting of three members, whose duty shall be to superintend and keep in good repair, the real estate and personal property which may be under the care of the Board. They shall not authorize any repairs that shall exceed the sum of fifty dollars, without first obtaining the approval of the Board.

SEC. 3. A Committee on Pews, consisting of three members, one of whom shall be the Pew Agent, who shall assist in the renting of pews and collecting pew rents.

SEC. 4. A Committee on Collections, consisting of at least six members, whose duty it shall be to take up the collections in the church, and hand the same to the Treasurer.

SEC. 5. A Committee on Sexton, consisting of three members, whose duty shall be to see that the Sexton discharges his duties in a proper manner, and attends to the proper heating and ventilation of the church.

SEC. 6. A Committee on Music, consisting of three members, whose duty shall be to superintend the Chorister and Organist in the discharge of their duties, so far as they come under the direction of the Board.

ARTICLE VI.

Election of Sexton, Chorister and Organist.

The Board shall elect by ballot, as occasion may require, suitable persons to serve as Sexton, Chorister and Organist, who shall receive for their services such salary as the Board may determine from time to time; the same to be paid quarterly.

ARTICLE VII.

Auditing Committee.

At the Stated Meeting in December, a Committee of three shall be appointed to audit the accounts of the Treasurer and Pew Agent, and prepare the annual report to the congregation.

ARTICLE VIII.

Vacancies.

The Board shall have power to fill all vacancies which may occur in their body by death, resignation or otherwise.

ARTICLE IX.

Alterations, additions or amendments to these By-Laws may be made by this Board, provided said alterations, &c., shall have been proposed in writing at least one month previous to acting thereon, and two-thirds of the members present concurring at the final decision.

APPENDIX.

After the manuscript copy of this history had passed into the hands of the publisher, and when some of the press-work had been completed, an unexpected endorsement was given to the writing, and publication of individual church history, by our General Assembly.

At its meeting held in Baltimore during the latter part of May, 1873, when the subject of the "Centennial celebration of American Independence" was under consideration, an animated and protracted discussion arose as to the wisdom and best mode of setting forth the progress of Presbyterianism in this country, during the last century.

Following this discussion, a number of resolutions were passed; among which, was one, in substance, recommending the pastors of the several churches under the jurisdiction of the assembly, to prepare and have published in time for the great Centennial Exhibition, to be held at Philadelphia in 1876, histories of their several churches, copies of which were to be sent to the Presbyterian Historical Society.

This action, while endorsing other actions referred

to in the prefatory article, has, in the publication of this volume not only been complied with, but anticipated.

As recorded in the body of this history, it was believed that the Salem German Reformed congregation which purchased our "old church building," intended to hold and occupy it for their own services. The most that was expected, was, that the building would be somewhat enlarged and remodeled, to afford ample accommodations for their very large membership.

Upon getting possession of the property, however, the people were undecided, as to what step to take. After waiting for some time, they rented it for a year to a congregation which had colonized from the Lutheran Church, at the corner of St. John and Brown streets. During this year, the renting congregation began and finished a church building in Fourth street, below Girard avenue.

The "old building" again vacated, was used at times for concerts and other entertainments, in behalf of the congregation to which it belonged. No pains were taken to keep it in repair, and, as a consequence, it became thoroughly dilapidated.

In the spring of 1873, the Salem congregation decided to build, and workmen about the beginning of

July, began to tear down the "old building," in order to make place for the "new."

The tearing down revealed the fact, that there was greater strength in the walls of the superstructure, than had previously been supposed; but it also showed a foundation *faulty*, because it partly rested on made ground.

Appearances indicated that when the church was erected, as much attention was given to the "burial vaults," as to the church edifice. There were twenty-six of these vaults; ten in front, and sixteen on the east side of the building.

As might have been inferred from the history, there was no "Corner-Stone." As already recorded, the building was erected by a "Stock Association," independent of any church organization. The formal transfer of the property to this congregation, did not take place for some time after the church had accepted the invitation of the "Association" to worship in their building.

It is the intention of the Salem congregation to erect a large edifice on the site of the old. They propose to adhere to the former *width*, but increase the *depth* of the building, by having the front some eight or ten feet nearer the street line, and placing the rear wall on the back line of their lot.

The work of building is now going on; and without attaching undue importance to time or place in our history, it will be pleasant in the future to remember that the spot where God in other days visited and blessed *us*, is still to invite like favors upon another Christian people, who are virtually one with us in doctrine and worship.

Were the words herein written only for the present, it would be needless to make mention of a *change in the name of the street*, on which the "Old Church" stood.

We would have thought no street name, more enduring than the name of Coates street. The present generation, at least, will hardly become familiarized with the new name given to that old thoroughfare.

But, recently our City Councils have ordered the old name on corners and street lamps to be taken down; and while *we* may read intelligibly the old and oft-repeated name of Coates street on these pages, hereafter, others to read satisfactorily, must substitute in the place of the old, the *new name*, FAIRMOUNT AVENUE.

We regret that we have not been able to secure a likeness of Rev. T. A. J. Mines, the second pastor of this church. Failure to secure, was not from want of effort. After much writing to those likely to have some reminder of him in picture, we are satisfied that no likeness of him can be had.

The likeness of the first pastor is taken from an oil painting now in possession of his widow, who lives at Princeton, N. J., while the others are lithographed from original photographs secured from themselves or from their friends, thus having their correctness endorsed. No better fac-simile of an autograph can be had than that which accompanies the several likenesses.

In closing this volume, I may be permitted to say that I have labored upon it, as opportunity offered, for more than a year. I claim for it no literary merit, but do assert its historical accuracy. Had I known in the beginning the amount of time, patience, research and correspondence required in its preparation, I would, to say the least, very reluctantly have commenced it.

Now that it is done, I am compensated by the discoveries I have made of the faith, hope, and self-sacrificing spirit of God's people, as I am also, and chiefly, by the oft-repeated testimony God has given in the history of this church, that he will never leave nor forsake those who put their trust in Him. To Him be glory and honor, both now and forever. Amen.

CONTENTS.

XII.

XIII.

ERRATA.

Page 15—15th line from the top, instead of *stone*, read *brick*.
" 70, 3d line from the bottom, instead of *dilapitated*, read *dilapidated*.
" 72, 11th line from the top, instead of *Messers.* read *Messrs.*
" 96, 8th line from the bottom, instead of *Whilden*, read *Whildin*.
" 121, 6th line from the top, instead of *Doman*, read *Dornan*.
" 123, 8th line from the bottom, instead of *Presbyteria*, read *Presbyterial*.
" 127, 2d line from the top, instead of *Craver*, read *Craven*.
" 137, 12th line from the bottom, instead of *Rev. G. W.*, read *Rev. G.*
" 167, 12th line from the top, instead of *one*, read *done*
" 201, 7th line from the bottom, instead of *Setwart*, read *Stewart*.
" 202, 7th line from the bottom, omit the *.
" 204, 4th line from the bottom, instead of *Eckhardt*, read *Erhardt*.
" 205, 8th line from the top, put * before A. H.
" 205, 5th line from the bottom, omit the *
" 210, 7th line from the bottom, put * before Robert
" 211, 2d line from the bottom, instead of *Mrs. J. W.*, read *Mrs. J. P.*

www.ingramcontent.com/pod-product-compliance
Lightning Source LLC
LaVergne TN
LVHW010241110826
845151LV00004B/1359

* 9 7 8 1 4 2 5 5 2 3 9 6 1 *